1993

a

happy christmas

love from

Jean

NOOKS AND CORNERS OF SHROPSHIRE

ARISE · PRAY · WORK
CRH

BUTCHER ROW,
SHREWSBURY.

Nooks and Corners

of

Shropshire.

BY

H. THORNHILL TIMMINS, F.R.G.S.,

AUTHOR OF 'NOOKS AND CORNERS OF HEREFORDSHIRE,' 'NOOKS AND CORNERS OF PEMBROKESHIRE.'

WITH MAP AND NUMEROUS ILLUSTRATIONS BY THE AUTHOR.

LONDON:
ELLIOT STOCK, 62, PATERNOSTER ROW, E.C.
1899.

Originally published in 1899
by Elliot Stock, London

0 9518589 2 0

Printed and bound by
Redwood Books, Trowbridge, Wiltshire
for
Lapridge Publications
25 Church Street, Hereford HR1 2LR
Telephone 0432 353586

PREFACE

Y work completed, I may be permitted to add a few words by way of envoi.

'Nooks and Corners' is the outcome of many prolonged sketching rambles in Shropshire, where, as I roamed about the County, in search of subjects for pen and pencil, I succeeded in gleaning a good deal of original information anent the places I visited; and I was greeted by all sorts and conditions of Salopians with that hospitality for which they are proverbial, and which has left me their grateful debtor.

Though the more important places here illustrated are probably familiar to many of my readers, there are certain scenes and objects in the course of this work which have never been pictured or described before, and which will, I trust, prove of interest to Salopians. Amidst such an embarras de richesses, I have of necessity been obliged to pick and choose the subjects dealt with; for in matter antiquarian the locality is well-nigh inexhaustible.

But if the gentle reader, in perusing the following pages, should share in some degree my own pleasure and interest in compiling them, I shall have the satisfaction of feeling that I have not rambled in vain amidst the Nooks and Corners of Shropshire.

H. THORNHILL TIMMINS.

HARROW,
November, 1899.

CONTENTS

INDEX TO ILLUSTRATIONS

NOOKS AND CORNERS OF SHROPSHIRE

'On this side whiche the Sonne doth warm with his declining beames,
Severn and Teme in channell deepe doo run, too antient Streames ;
These make the neibor's pasture riche, these yeld of fruit greate store ;
And doo convey thro out the Shire commodities manie more.
Here hilles doo lift their heades aloft, from whence sweete springes doo flow,
Whose moistur good doth firtil make the vallies coucht belowe.
Here goodly orchards planted are, in fruite which doo abounde ;
Thine ey wold make thine hart rejoyce to see such pleasant grounde.'

A GENERAL SURVEY. THE TOWN OF SHREWSBURY.

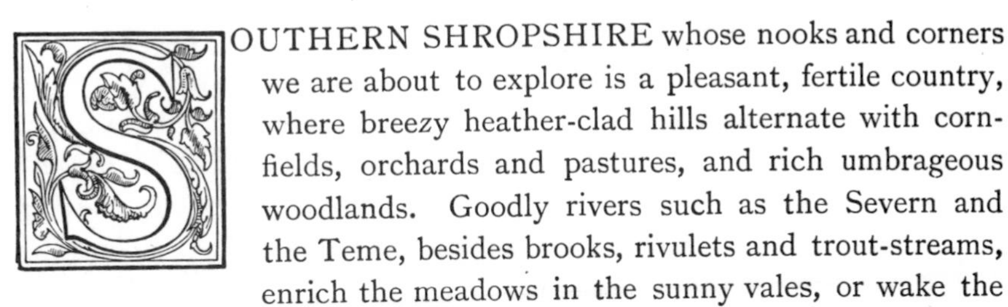

SOUTHERN SHROPSHIRE whose nooks and corners we are about to explore is a pleasant, fertile country, where breezy heather-clad hills alternate with corn-fields, orchards and pastures, and rich umbrageous woodlands. Goodly rivers such as the Severn and the Teme, besides brooks, rivulets and trout-streams, enrich the meadows in the sunny vales, or wake the silence of the lonely hills where the curlew and the lapwing make their homes.

Situated upon the confines of England and Wales, this border district forms part of the March-lands which in olden times sundered the realm of England from the Principality, and hence one may enjoy within its comparatively moderate compass the diversified scenery peculiar to either country. As regards its physical features, therefore, Southern Shropshire presents in some sort an epitome or microcosm of England itself.

A glance at the map will show that the whole south-western corner of Shropshire is occupied by the wild hill-country known as Clun Forest; whence a succession of lofty ridges, such as the Stiperstones, the Longmynd, the Caradoc Hills and Wenlock Edge, ramificate towards the north, in shape not unlike the fingers of a hand, whereof the Clee Hills, lying a little apart to the eastward, may be taken as representing the thumb.

This hilly region is classic ground to the geologist. The extreme diversity of its rock structure early attracted the attention of students; and has been so thoroughly elucidated by Murchison, Ramsay, Salter, Lapworth, and other eminent scientists, that nowadays as the saying goes 'he who runs may read.'

The Severn is *the* river par excellence of Shropshire. With its important affluent the Teme, this noble river, in its course of more than fifty miles through the county, receives the waters of the entire district. After parting company with the rugged hills of Wales, the Severn emerges upon the plains of Shropshire, and sweeps in a bold curve around the town of Shrewsbury. Thenceforth the ever-widening river glides onward in placid reaches past the time-honoured ruins of Roman Uriconium, and lingers beside lush green water meadows, where the ruddy kine stand knee-deep in the rippling shallows, and the salmon fisher drifts by in his coracle as he spreads his nets athwart stream.

Anon the Severn, changing its character, plunges along in eddying rapids beneath the limestone escarpments of Benthall and Wenlock Edge; then, taking a southerly trend, it skirts the groves and terraces of Apley Park, washes the walls of picturesque old Bridgnorth, and finally the big river takes leave of our county amidst the rough holts and heaths of that ancient woodland which goes by the name of Wyre Forest.

Owing to the lie of the land, the more important streams of

Southern Shropshire flow, not into the Severn itself, but into its tributary the Teme. The northern Rea, the Cound and the Worf, it is true, find their way direct to the former river; but the waters of the Clun, the Onny, the Ledwych and the southern Rea, go to swell the tide of the Teme.

Dividing the county of Salop from its neighbour Herefordshire, the river Teme pursues a devious course through some of the most delightful scenery in all these broad March-lands. From its lonely source amidst the hills, away beyond the Welsh border, the infant Teme comes tumbling and prattling along beneath the rolling heights of Clun Forest, and, passing onwards to Ludlow, meanders beside the castle walls, and flows in a graceful arc around the rocky slopes of Whitcliff. Near Tenbury the Teme travels into Worcestershire, which it does not quit again until it merges its waters in those of the Severn.

With all these varied attractions, its picturesque rural landscapes, its old-world towns and villages fraught with memories of the past, and the thousand-and-one sights, scents and sounds, that go to make up the indefinable charm of an English countryside, the visitor to Shropshire may find ample opportunity to gratify his particular taste, or pursue his favourite hobby, be it that of an artist, a sportsman, a botanist, or a votary of the 'gentle art'; while for the cyclist, and in a still greater measure for him who fares afoot, there lurks many a secluded nook in the unfrequented byways, or amidst the hollows of the silent hills; nooks where he may enjoy to heart's content the harvest of the quiet eye.

From the antiquarian point of view, Shropshire is exceptionally interesting. Britons, Romans, Danes, Saxons and Normans, have all played their parts in moulding its early history, and have graven upon the natural features of the country indelible traces of their former domination.

That Shropshire shared to the full in the drum and trumpet history of mediæval days, is attested by the ruined castles and strongholds to be met with on every hand. These we shall have occasion to refer to in the course of our rambles; so turn we now to the famous old town which forms the centre and focus of Salopian life.

* * * * * *

Just about the middle of the county, islanded almost by a bold southward sweep of the Severn, stands Shrewsbury, the Pengwern of the old Welsh days, the Saxon Scrobbesbyrig; an ancient borough town and the capital of the district. Shrewsbury is a clean, cheerful, yet withal picturesque-looking city, where the tide of modern progress rolls to and fro along the steep old streets beside its ancient castle, past venerable parish churches and the quaint, half-timbered mansions of the ancienne noblesse.

Hotels and lodging-houses are not far to seek, while highroads and lines of railway ramificate from Shrewsbury throughout the county; so the traveller who intends to explore the nooks and corners of the surrounding district cannot do better than take up his quarters for a time in the proud old city upon Severn side.

The topography of Shrewsbury is tolerably simple. Encompassed on all sides save the north by the noble river Severn, the town spreads away up a gentle hill to the walls of its guardian castle. 'The Towne of Shrewesbury,' says John Leland, 'standeth on a Rocky Hill of Stone of a sad redde Earth, and Severne soe girdeth in all the Towne that, saving a little Peice, it were an Isle.'

Right through the centre of the city, from south-east towards the west, runs the ancient highroad, or 'reddie way,' from London to North Wales; entering by way of the English Bridge, passing through the town under the names of Wyle Cop, High Street and Mardol, and emerging by the Welsh Bridge. At right angles to this thoroughfare lies Castle Street, leading up to the gates of the old Norman stronghold, and nowadays familiar to travellers as the road to the railway-station. Castle Street leads on to Pride Hill, one of the busiest arteries of the city, which in its turn is prolonged down St. John's Hill to the Quarry, a public park shaded by avenues of lofty lime trees, affording a pleasant stroll by Severn side. Here, some three centuries ago, Churchyard the Shropshire poet beheld:

'A space belowe to bait both Bull and Beare ;
For players, too, great roume, and place at will,
And in the same a Cockpit, wondrous fayre,
Besides, where men may wrestle in their fill.'

Across the river rises Shrewsbury School, the handsome modern prototype of the older foundation in the town, encompassed by spacious demesnes and cricket fields, the scene in bygone times of the far-famed 'Shrewsbury Show.' Abbey Foregate, with its venerable monastic

church, occupies what may be called the English side of the city; while the ancient suburb of Frankwell climbs the hill in a westerly direction, away beyond the Welsh Bridge.

* * * * * *

We now set forth on a peregrination of the town, keeping an eye lifting for such relics of the past as may lie upon our road, and remarking the quaint nomenclature of some of the older streets. Immediately as we step outside the railway-station, the old city gives us a taste of its quality; for yonder rise the ruddy sandstone walls and round-towers of Shrewsbury Castle, 'built in such a brave Plott,' as an old writer observes, 'that it could have espyed a Byrd flying in every Streete.'

Originally erected by the all-powerful Roger de Montgomery, all that now remains of the feudal castle is a Norman gateway, two massive drum-towers of the Edwardian keep, and some remnants of the inner ward or bailey. So long ago as Henry the Eighth's time, John Leland found the fortress 'nowe much in ruine,' and although its ancient walls were furbished up, and a garrison put in charge to hold the place for King Charles, it was delivered by treachery into the hands of the Parliamentarian forces, and so escaped demolition.

Turning uphill into Castle Gates, we espy a flight of steps leading to a sort of raised passage, called the Dana, whence the visitor, if so minded, may survey a large portion of Shropshire. Returning now to Castle Gates, we bend our steps towards a dignified-looking pile of grey stone buildings, standing a little back from the roadway.

This is the Free Library and Museum, a building that for some three centuries did duty as the Grammar School of Shrewsbury; a school founded by King Edward the Sixth, enlarged by Queen Elizabeth, and numbering among its masters men like Dr. Samuel Butler and Kennedy of Cambridge, and made famous by such scholars as Philip Sidney, Fulk Greville and Darwin, not to mention in the same breath the execrable name of Judge Jeffreys.

Before the entrance gateway, which is adorned with the effigies of two scholars in quaint Jacobean costume, stands the recently erected bronze statue of Charles Darwin, the world-renowned scientist, an alumnus, and a native of Shrewsbury.

The interior of the building proves quite in keeping with what the outside would lead one to expect, for the low-ceiled rooms, with their dark oaken panelling and doors carved with the names of long-forgotten schoolboys, seem redolent of scholarly ways; and these studious traditions are in some sense maintained by the purposes which these quiet chambers now serve.

Once more we steer a diagonal course athwart steep, crowded

Castle Street, and, rounding the end of a modern chapel, find ourselves immediately vis-à-vis the object of our search. An ancient archway, surmounted by a pair of timbered gablets, admits us to a small paved courtyard, around three sides of which extends a group of buildings, which in bygone days formed the Council House, and occasional abode of no less a personage than the Lord President of the Council of the Marches of Wales. Many a stately ceremony has doubtless graced hese venerable precincts, which still impress the visitor with their look of faded dignity, though fallen in these latter days from their honourable estate, and converted to the purposes of private dwelling-houses.

The picturesque Gate House, however, which figures in our sketch may very well have witnessed that memorable incident in Shrewsbury's corporate history, when the sturdy burgesses refused Charles the First's offer (while staying at the Council House in 1642) to create their town a city, an occasion that earned for them ever after the title of 'Proud Salopians.' This fine old Gate House has been but little altered, and bears upon its ancient timbers the date A.D. 1620. An old hall to the rear still retains its original oak panelling and chimney-piece, charged with fantastic devices, and dated 1634; while an upper chamber contains a massive oak tester-bedstead, whose richly carved top is supported by moulded pillars.

Pushing onward past Plimmer's, formerly Palin's, home of the famous cake-compounder whose praises have been sung by Thomas Ingoldsby Esq., we come to the trim façade of the Raven Hotel, a commodious hostelry whose fame goes back far into the old coaching days. Then, espying a lofty steeple peering over the nearer housetops, we cross the head of the lane by which Cromwell's men made their way into the town, and enter the little green close where stands St. Mary's Church.

Built of mellow-hued, weatherworn sandstone, St. Mary's proves to be a noble cruciform edifice, with an early south porch and parvise, and one of the finest spires in all England. The interior, too, presents a charming diversity, from the variety of architectural styles employed, and is spanned by a panelled oaken ceiling richly and beautifully wrought; while the spacious 'Jesse' window in the chancel, brought from old Grey Friars monastery, affords a combination of sweetness and light truly pleasant to behold. Indeed, the ancient glass in St. Mary's Church forms quite a feature of the building; and amidst its quaint imagery St. Bernard may be detected in the act of sweeping the excommunicated flies out of church, and a representation of the Last Judgment with Satan figuring as a blue boar!

Amongst other interesting monuments of greater or less antiquity, we notice a memorial to that skilled and daring seaman Admiral Benbow, a renowned Salopian hero, and 'true patterne of English courage,' who died at Jamaica from honourable wounds in 1702.

Beneath the shadow of St. Mary's Church nestles a group of lowly almshouses, a charity established some time prior to 1648. Yonder ancient half-timbered gable, overlooking the churchyard, is the erstwhile Hall of the Drapers' Guild, where, upon passing within, we find ourselves in a spacious, low-ceiled chamber, entirely wainscoted with oak, and having massive oak tables, benches and lockers, coeval with the room. Upon the wall hangs a dark old panel-picture, commonly supposed to be the portrait of Degory Watur, the founder, and his lady wife, who, it is recorded, used to attend with the ministers 'dailye in Our Ladye's Churche, and kneele with them in a long Pewe, in the guise made for them and himselfe.' And the old bedesman who does the honours also displays one or two ancient charters connected with the foundation, which are jealously preserved here under lock and key.

Passing on to Pride Hill—so named from a local family of that ilk who lived in a mansion hard by—we presently descry a narrow thoroughfare, looking for all the world like a bit of some mediæval city. This is Butcher Row, a quaint, old-time byway, whose ancient timbered houses lean this way or that, in sociable good-fellowship, above the little shops that flank the lane. A sketch of Butcher Row forms the frontispiece to this volume.

'There they stand, crowding together, with overhanging gables, queer dormer windows, and panelled fronts; a curious chequer-work, wherein the broad black lines are displayed upright, horizontal and diagonal, with varied artifice. And here and there a bracket catches the eye, or a pent-house roof and railed recesses, and breadths of ornament on fascia and cornice. The ground-floors recede, and shops are gloomy, and ceilings low; and upstairs you find the same want of height and breadth of window, by which the olden time contrived to favour at once the picturesque, and the plague.'

Far aloft soars the graceful spire of St. Alkmund's Church, ('Stalkmun's,' in the vernacular), the nave whereof was pulled down in a panic a century ago, after its neighbour St. Chad's had fallen, and rebuilt in the contemptible 'style' of that period.

'In the yere 1533,' as an old chronicler tells, 'uppon Twelffe daye, in Shrowsburie, the Dyvyll appearyd in Saint Alkmond's churche there, when the Preest was at High Masse, with great tempeste and Darknesse, soe that as he passyd through, he mountyd upp the Steeple in the sayd churche, tering the wyers of the clocke, and put the prynt of his Clawes uppon the 4th Bell, and tooke one of the pynnacles awaye with hym, and for the Tyme stayde all the Bells in the churches within the sayde Towne, that they could neyther toll nor ringe.'

The corner building at the farther end of Butcher Row is an excellent example of a mediæval town-house; and the beautiful though sadly defaced carvings about its door-jambs, windows and gables, are as good as they are rare of their kind. There is reason to suppose the Abbots of Lilleshall made this their city abode, and that the chantry priests of the Holy Cross found shelter in its ancient chambers.

Be that as it may, we now direct our steps towards a mere slit of a passage, aptly designated Grope Lane; getting a passing peep of Fish Street, and its quaint inn-sign the Three Fishes, the cognizance of the Abbots of Lilleshall, with St. Julian's Church-tower beyond. A queer nook indeed is this Grope Lane, just such an one as might have inspired the author of 'A Legend of the Dark Entry'; so narrow that one may easily touch both sides at once, and so closely overhung by the rafters of the adjacent premises that but a strip of sky is seen.

Having weathered the intricacies of Grope Lane we enter High Street, and turn right-about to look at the quaint old half-timbered buildings by which it is flanked—small but very characteristic specimens of old Salopian house-fronts, with their quatrefoil panels, twisted pilasters, and grotesquely carved heads. Close at hand is High Street Church, a chapel originally erected in the days of the Act of Uniformity, and noteworthy from the fact that for a brief space of time Samuel Coleridge, the celebrated author of the 'Ancient Mariner,' ministered therein.

Strolling along High Street, we soon pass the entrance to The Square, giving a passing glance at the old Market House that rises so picturesquely there—whereof more anon,—and pausing beneath Clive's statue to scan the determined features and stalwart bearing of that renowned Salopian. Then we turn our attention to a group of fine old black-and-white gables that rise upon the opposite side of the street the doorway of one handsome façade bearing the inscription, ERECTED BY RICHARD OWEN THE ELDER, GENTELMAN, ANO. DM. 1592.

REMAINS OF BENNETT'S HALL

Few towns in the kingdom can boast such stately survivals as these; yet a few yards away appears a still more striking specimen of the mediæval builder's art. Originally the town-house of the Irelands, this noble old fabric is still known by their name, and bears upon its ancient front the family cognizance. Four storeys high it rears its chequered walls, topped by tall, beetling gables, and broken into play of light and shade by ranges of oriel windows. Bits of quaint carving are seen here and there upon bargeboard, lintel and bracket, for the old place has happily suffered but little from modern innovations. The nicely restored black-and-white front of Lloyd's Bank hard by keeps its venerable neighbour well in countenance.

Finding ourselves once more on Pride Hill, we step across that busy thoroughfare, and, passing to the rear of Mother Noblett's Toffee Shop, with its huge, comical signboard, we see before us the pretty

Gothic doorway that figures in our sketch. Though much the worse for neglect, and fallen sadly into disrepair, this ancient sandstone structure is clearly the work of at least two periods. The shaft and capital on the left, with the broken archway above it, are of the style known as Early English; while the graceful pointed arch, with its floreated cusps and traces of ball-flower ornamentation, are evidently a later insertion, and probably date from the latter part of the thirteenth century. A wide stone arch, part of which may be noticed above the passage-way, supports the floor of the room within; and a small arched recess, near the head of the steps, appears to have been used as a holy-water stoup.

From these indications it is considered probable the little building before us was at one time the private chapel of Bennett's Hall, the city residence of the Abbot of Haughmond, who, according to the custom of those days, had a town-house in the capital of the county.

Portions of ancient domestic buildings may be traced at the back of the chapel, including the stonework of a good-sized hall, and some indications of a large window. There is a tradition that these buildings were at one time used as a mint; and the fact that a kind of oven, or hearth, formerly existed here gives colour to the story.

Laying a course towards the tall clock-tower of the new Market Hall, we now descend Pride Hill and turn to the right into Mardol, a steep, oldfashioned street, boasting several half-timbered house-fronts dating as far back as the fifteenth and sixteenth centuries. About half-way down we strike into a byway called Hill's Lane, at the corner whereof rises an ancient frontage whose oaken beams display the date 1440. This narrow lane, zig-zagging through one of the oldest quarters of the town, is frequented on market-days by country folk, when the mother-tongue of old Salopia may be heard in all its pristine purity.

After passing one or two oldfashioned inns of the humbler sort, we stumble unexpectedly upon a lordly dwelling, standing somewhat aloof from its dingy neighbours, and presenting an air of dilapidated

A BYEWAY IN OLD SHREWSBURY.

gentility, like an out-at-elbows aristocrat making shift to maintain his dignity amidst a crowd of tatterdemalions.

Built of dark-red brick, with stone mullions, quoins and copings, this fine old Tudor mansion is believed to have been erected by one William Rowley, draper, and sometime alderman of Shrewsbury, about the beginning of the seventeenth century, and is still called Rowley's Mansion. Sad it is to see the woful plight into which the stately old fabric has fallen, the beautiful porch that once adorned its entrance torn away and destroyed, its mullioned windows yawning wide to wind and rain, and each delicately-traceried ceiling thrown down, or utterly defaced. By strolling into the yard of the old Ship Inn, we get another glimpse of Rowley's mansion; its soaring gables and chimney stacks grouping picturesquely, from this point, with the meaner outhouses and dwellings by which it is surrounded.

We next thread our way through several rather intricate lanes, until, crossing Mardol Head, we soon find ourselves once more in The Square, the very heart of this ancient city. Here the old Market House at once claims our attention; a venerable sandstone structure supported, as our sketch will show, upon a series of semicircular arches, and buttressed at the angles. Overhead its time-stained walls are pierced with mullioned windows, and relieved against the skyline by quaint, fantastic battlements. That clock aloft in the gable is *said* to occupy the place of the one Falstaff referred to when declaring that, against tremendous odds, he had 'fought a long hour by Shrewsbury clock.' Be that as it may, we are on surer ground when considering the figure in the canopied niche below; for an inscribed panel alongside announces that 'This statue was removed by order of the Mayor from the tower on the Welsh Bridge in the year 1791.' The effigy, that of a knight in full armour, has a stiff, archaic appearance, and is usually supposed to represent Edward IV., father of Richard, Duke of York. Below this figure, in antiquated characters, are the words: THE XV DAY OF IUNE WAS THIS BUYLDING BEGONN, W^M^ JONES AND THOS. CHARLTON GENT. THEN BAYLIFFES, AND WAS ERECTED AND COVERED IN THEIR TIME. The opposite gable has a similar niche, with the figure of an angel bearing a shield charged with the Arms of England and France, and a half-obliterated sundial. A richly carved canopy upon the western front encloses the arms of Queen Elizabeth, and the date of the erection of the building, 1596.

Over against the old Market House, on the eastern side of The Square, rises an ancient timbered dwelling which goes by the name of Lloyd's House. Its rugged beams are curiously carved; grotesque faces leer upon the passer-by from finial and bracket; and the builder's initials are ingeniously interwoven amidst the ornamentation of the weatherworn bargeboard. Glancing backwards from the adjacent lane, we notice how the nodding gables and chimneys of Lloyd's mansion, one end of the old Market House, and a good eighteenth-century building beyond, combine to form a characteristic street scene. Then we push onwards again in search of other quarry.

Traversing a disused cemetery, we come to the Lady Chapel, and only relic, of old St. Chad's, a venerable church which collapsed suddenly in 1788, after surviving the changes and chances of time, it is said, for over a thousand years.

An odd little alley now beguiles our footsteps, where an old-fashioned inn, its prominent signboard overtopped by St. Julian's church-tower, appears as set in a frame beneath an ancient archway. Thence we turn to the right, and pass a handsome new building on the site of Shearmen's Hall, an ancient foundation that in its time had played many parts, as a theatre, a chapel, a warehouse and a shop!

Thus we enter Wyle Cop,—how runs the verse?

> 'They hew, and they hack, and they chop;
> And, to finish the whole, they stick up a pole,
> In the place that's still called the Wylde Coppe,
> And they pop
> Your grim, gory head on the top!'

Several attractive-looking old structures confront us as we descend the steep pavement, prominent amongst them the ancient abode that figures upon page 15. This picturesque façade, with its

OLD MARKET HOUSE
SHREWSBURY.

Old Houses in Wyle Cop, Shrewsbury.

blackened timbers and pretty traceried window adorned by coats of arms, has an added interest from the fact that it is 'Ye auncient house in which King Henry the VII loged, when he went to Bosworth Field, Augst 1485.' So at least the panel beneath the window has it, though Henry, of course, was but Harry of Richmond until that fateful battle had won for him the crown.

While exploring the vicinity of Wyle Cop, many another bit of old Shrewsbury is brought to light, notably the nicely restored frontage of the Unicorn Hotel; and, hidden away amidst some poor cottages by Severn side, a few scanty relics of Grey Friars' monastery, in its time one of the stateliest religious houses in Shrewsbury. Thenceforward we hug the river brink until, coming to the English Bridge, we traverse it, and find ourselves in the broad thoroughfare called Abbey Foregate—

> 'A long greate streate, well buildid, large and faire,
> In as good Ayre as may be wisht with wit ;
> Where Abbey stands, and is such ringe of Belles,
> As is not found from London unto Welles.'

These lines by Churchyard, the old Shropshire poet, still hold good in the main, though railway encroachments have much to answer for. But the pièce de résistance is happily still there, and the ruddy, time-worn tower of the Abbey Church now rises before us, while its mellow-toned bells speak for themselves, pealing out a quaint, merry chime upon the springlike air as we draw near.

Originally amongst the noblest and wealthiest Abbeys of the Benedictine order in England, this venerable edifice remains to this day one of the few ancient religious houses in everyday use as a parish church. It was founded by no less a personage than Roger de Montgomery, William the Conqueror's kinsman and vicegerent in the Welsh March-lands; who, life's fitful fever ended, lies buried here in his own Abbey Church of St. Peter and St. Paul.

Earl Roger's foundation was probably cruciform in shape, and the central portion of the church is part of the original fabric, displaying the thick, massive pillars and rounded arches, characteristic of the Norman period. In pleasant contrast with their rude simplicity rises a group of gracefully proportioned, pointed arches of a later date; while the tall, slender traceries of the Perpendicular windows, lend a certain air of lightness to the whole. A flat oaken ceiling spans the lofty interior, which cannot fail to impress every beholder by its air of spacious and reposeful dignity.

In the south aisle we notice a recumbent and much defaced stone effigy, which, according to a brass plate upon the adjacent wall, represents 'Sir Roger de Montgomery, Second in command of the army of his kinsman, William the Conqueror, at the Battle of Hastings, the First of the Family of Montgomery in England. He was advanced to high honour as the Over-lord of many counties, and created Earl of Shrewsbury. He founded this church and abbey, wherein he, as a Brother of the Benedictine Order, died the 1st of August, MXCV.' The monuments in the Abbey Church will reward a close examination.

Ancient Pulpit
at Shrewsbury.

In the course of a walk around the outside of the church, we remark the noble proportions of the great west window, surmounted by a canopied niche, with its mailed figure reputed to represent King Edward III., a picturesque two-storied north porch, and the lofty walls of Mr. Pearson's new chancel. Thence we pass across the street, where, a pathetic object amidst such grimy environments, stands the ancient stone pulpit shown in our sketch, in the midst of a railway coal-yard!

This graceful structure dates from the early part of the fourteenth century, and its cusped and richly moulded arches are charming examples of Decorated work. The panels below are adorned with delicately sculptured figures representing St. Peter, St. Paul, and other saints; while the groined ceiling inside the arches is crowned by a large carved boss, or keystone, emblematical of the Crucifixion.

Very picturesque looks this gem of Gothic art, its grey old stones scored and wrinkled by the tooth of Time, whose ravages are but partially concealed by a mantle of fresh green ivy. At one time the Abbey precincts appear to have extended far and wide in this direction, but the exigencies of modern travel and traffic have played sad havoc with the old, monkish habitation.

This beautiful pulpit is the last remnant of the old monastic buildings, that once nestled beneath the adjacent Abbey Church. It was attached to the refectory, and was doubtless intended for the use of the monk whose duty it was to read to the brethren at meal-times. Its other side gave upon the courtyard of the monastery, and we may suppose that open-air sermons were occasionally delivered from it.

Our sketch completed, we now turn aside from Abbey 'Forrit,' to visit the large red sandstone mansion, paradoxically dubbed 'White-hall.' It is recorded that Richard Prince, its builder, commenced the erection of his house in the year of grace 1578, but that it was not completed until 1582, 'soe was it iiij yeares in buyldinge, to hys greate chardge, with fame to hym and hys posteritie for ever.' Prince's 'fame' in the matter is somewhat discounted, however, by the fact that he built his dwelling with stones torn from the fabric of the ancient Abbey, then but lately disestablished; and, in order to disguise them, caused the walls to be whitewashed, which gave rise to its name of Whitehall.

The building is a very fine specimen of an Elizabethan mansion, with mullioned windows, high-peaked gables, and the tall, detached chimney-stacks one knows so well. The gatehouse and dovecot are interesting features, and the lawn at the rear of the mansion is overshadowed by a magnificent walnut tree, as old, we should suppose, as Whitehall itself.

We now push on to St. Giles's Church, turning aside to climb to the summit of Lord Hill's Column, and enjoy the wide and varied prospect over hill and dale, town and river, that its balcony affords.

St. Giles's is considered to be one of the oldest churches in Shrewsbury; yet, owing to repeated restoration—'a name that,' as has been well said, 'covers more sins than charity itself,'—a casual observer might easily mistake it for a brand-new edifice. The church owes its foundation, we believe, to King Henry I., who established here a hospital or asylum for lepers, of whom St. Giles was regarded as the special patron. A Norman doorway admits us to the interior, which, though rigorously swept and garnished, still retains one or two of its original windows filled with scraps of ancient stained glass, and a richly moulded archway of rather later date.

Out in the churchyard stands a curious octagonal stone, with a good-sized square recess, several inches deep, in its upper side. It is known as the Pest Basin, and dates from the days when the plague was raging in Shrewsbury, during the seventeenth century. The custom was for the townsfolk to cast their money into the water in this basin, whence it was taken out by the country people in payment for the 'loaves and fishes' they supplied, thus avoiding in some sort the risk of actual contagion.

One of the tombstones here is inscribed with the following laconic legend:

'Here Charles Rathbon hee doth lie
And by misfortun hee did dye
On the 17th of July—1751.'

Through the quiet of the gloaming we now wend our way townwards again, the roofs and steeples of old Shrewsbury showing darkly silhouetted against the golden west as we cross the English Bridge. Thereafter, over a pipe in the chimney-nook of our hostelry, we fall to 'babbling o' green fields' and poring over Ordnance maps, intending on the morrow's morn to quit these scenes of our 'daily walks and ancient neighbourhood,' and fare forth into the open country.

FROM SHREWSBURY TO PITCHFORD, ACTON BURNELL, AND CHURCH STRETTON.

A SILVERY mackerel sky, serene and calm, gives promise of a bright Spring day, as, drawn by the iron horse, we spin along betwixt fields and hedgerows en route for Dorrington Station.

Half-way out we skirt the wooded slopes of Lythwood, once upon a time a royal forest, whence Henry the Third permitted the Hospitallers of St. Giles's to draw wood for their firing. Presently the gently-flowing river Cound is seen, travelling Severn-wards through a pleasant, agricultural country; and then, detraining at the next station, we shoulder our knapsacks and trudge away in the direction of Stapleton.

Old hawthorn hedges fling their scented sprays athwart the dusty highway, and the verdant wheat-fields beyond them are fringed with feathery cow's-parsley, looking for all the world like green carpets edged with white lace. The oaks are beating the ash trees this Spring in their race for precedence, and in yonder grounds a copper beech rears its magnificent purple dome against the deep blue of the sky—a sight for sair e'en!

Arrived at Stapleton church, we notice that it appears to consist of two separate and distinct churches, the one superposed upon the other; the two having been at some past time united by removing the floor of the upper one, giving to the interior somewhat the appearance of a college chapel.

The lower portion of the fabric, with its thick, massive walls and curiously narrow windows, mere loops, appears to be of early Norman

date; while the plain lancet lights above might belong to the early part of the thirteenth century. On the south side of the chancel is a

CONDOVER HALL
SHROPSHIRE
H.T.T

pair of two-light windows filled with simple tracery, and between them is seen the door that formerly gave entrance to the upper church. Near to the latter is an arched recess, which it has been conjectured was originally a nativity grotto. Farther east upon the same wall rises the pretty sedilia, surmounted by the double cusped arch seen on the right in the adjoining view. There are little trefoil lights under these arches, but they are later insertions.

Upon the pulpit hangs an antipendium, worked in gold and silver thread with a beautiful scrolly pattern, which, if we are to credit the local tradition, was wrought by the hands of Mary, Queen of Scots. An Easter sepulchre, invisible in our sketch, is in the wall beyond; and the two tall processional candlesticks on either side the altar are exotics here, having been brought, it is said, from Nuremberg, in Germany. They are excellent specimens of Gothic wood-carving, and are richly coloured and gilt.

Returning into the highroad, we follow it for about a mile, and then strike away to the right through leafy bylanes that land us eventually at Condover, a pleasant, rural-looking village, almost encircled by the waters of the little river Cound.

Near the entrance to the village stands a very ancient dwelling-house, built after the manner of a ship turned keel upwards; the huge oak beams that support both walls and roof curving upwards from the ground, and passing through both storeys to meet at the ridge-pole.

Presently we come to the parish church, a large stone edifice surrounded by luxuriant foliage, and espy, hard by the churchyard wicket, an old derelict font doing duty as a flower-vase. The transepts are evidently of Norman date; while the nave and the fine west tower, though they look considerably older, were built no longer ago than the middle of the seventeenth century.

From the church we pass on to Condover Hall, a noble structure of the Elizabethan period, situated on the outskirts of the village. Viewed through the tall entrance gateway, the old mansion, with its picturesque gables, stone-mullioned windows and clustered chimney-stacks, presents a delightfully old-world appearance, which is enhanced by the quaintly clipped shrubs flanking the broad carriage-drive.

The west front, shown in a neighbouring sketch, overlooks a wide tract of park land, studded with gnarled hawthorns and ancient oaks, and watered by the meanderings of the stream whence the place derives its name.

The estate of Condover having been originally purchased by his father, Thomas of that ilk, Sir Roger Owen, in the year 1598, erected the existing mansion; calling in master Walter Hancocke, a celebrated craftsman of that period, to assist in planning his residence.

Condover passed in after years to the Cholmondeleys, an ancient family in whose hands the estate continued for many generations, having only recently been disposed of, and its interesting treasures dispersed.

We now push on for Pitchford, striking the main road at a place called Cantlop Cross, and following it until we get a glimpse of the old mansion itself, seated on a verdant slope amidst masses of shadowy foliage. A winding pathway, overarched by beech trees and ancestral oaks, meanders through the park, and leads us down to a low stone bridge, where we pause awhile to enjoy the charming view of Pitchford Hall, which our artist has portrayed.

Built by William Ottley, Sheriff of Shropshire, in the early part of the seventeenth century, Pitchford Hall remains a beautiful and interesting example of an old English homestead of that period. Nothing can exceed the picturesqueness of this venerable house, its weather-stained walls chequered by oaken timbers, its solid stone-tiled roofs carpeted with lichens and moss, and surmounted by huge crumbling chimney-stacks of curious design. Embosomed amidst tall trees and luxuriant shrubberies, with a lordly peacock taking the air upon the sunny terrace, and a clear stream whimpling along at our feet, the scene is one to be remembered; such an one, indeed, as this rural England of ours alone can shew.

But let us take a nearer look at the old Hall. The building, after the custom then in vogue, is fashioned like a capital E, the shorter member being represented by a central gable of very unusual appearance, containing a curious clock. By the courtesy of Lieut.-Colonel Cotes, the present proprietor, we are enabled to examine the interesting features of the interior, which contains some notable ancestral portraits, and a singular sort of picture-map showing the Hall and grounds as they existed in 1682. In one wainscoted chamber our attention is directed to a secret closet, or hidie-hole, ingeniously disguised by a sliding panel very difficult to detect; indeed, every corner of the mansion has its interest for the antiquary.

After having been the seat of the Ottley family for considerably more than three centuries, Pitchford Hall passed in the year 1807 into the possession of the late Lord Liverpool, who had the honour of entertaining Her Majesty here when, as Princess Victoria, she visited in this locality with the Duchess of Kent, in the year of the great Reform Bill.

Before taking leave of Pitchford, we pass out into the grounds to visit the so-called House in the Tree. As shewn in the picture here, this consists of a small chamber, about 9 or 10 feet square, and covered with a peaked roof—not much in itself, yet curious from the fact that it is built, high and dry, aloft in the fork of a huge old storm-rent lime tree, and is approached by a crooked flight of steps. Tradition avers that a 'house' has existed in this tree any time these two centuries past, having been formerly used as a dwelling; and the broken stump of more than one huge limb shews how severe have been the gales this venerable lime tree has weathered.

Upon a slight eminence hard by the mansion rises Pitchford church, a plain, simple structure, evidently of great antiquity. Built into its southern wall we notice a rude stone slab, apparently older than the church itself, with a raised cross enclosed by a circle cut in low relief upon its surface. An otherwise ordinary-looking interior is relieved by the handsome, recumbent effigy, of which a sketch will be found on p. 41. This remarkable monument is entirely composed of oak, black and smooth as ebony from lapse of time. The figure, some 7 feet in length, is that of a Crusader, habited in chain-mail, the hands clasping a sword, and the spurred feet resting upon a couchant dog, or talbot. Upon the base of the structure are seven trefoil arches, enclosing shields charged with armorial bearings, all excellently wrought, and in a good state of preservation. From its general character there can be no doubt this monument is of very early date; indeed it is supposed to represent Sir Ralph de Pitchford, who died in 1252.

Retracing our steps to the bridge, let us turn aside there for a moment to look at the ancient Pitch Well, a feature probably unique of its kind, whence the adjacent Hall derives its name.

The Well proves to be a largish shallow affair of an oval shape, and about 2 feet in depth, while the surface of the well (which is almost dried up this drouthy season) has little 'pockets' of semi-liquid pitch, oozing up from below and partially caked on the top. This bituminous spring appears, indeed, to have altered but little since Marmaduke Rawdon visited the spot, during a tour in the seventeenth century. 'Thir is in this Well,' he observes, 'foure littel Hooles about a halfe yard diep, out of whiche comes lyttle lumpes of Pitche, but that which is att y^e^ tope of y^e^ Well is softish, and swimes uppon the

Pitchford Hall.

water like Tarr, butt being skym'd together itt incorporateth, and is knead together like untoo soft wax, and becometh harde.'

Sketches completed, we now make for the village, and pace on through the quiet, weedgrown street, where the martins are nesting under the lee of the old stone-tiled roofs, and the still, sunny air is redolent of lilac and early honeysuckle. Yonder gable-end with its rough yellow plasterwork, venetian shutters, and mantle of purple wistaria, greets the eye with a pleasant scheme of colour, calling up visions of far-away Italy.

Thus we take the road again, until, coming to a green, grassy lane —part of the ancient Watling Street—we proceed to follow it up. At a point where the lane crosses a streamlet between hollow, sandy banks, we find unmistakable traces of a very ancient stone bridge, which, though undermined by rabbit burrows and damaged by tangled roots and brushwood, still shews the springing of a massive arch, apparently of semicircular form, while tumbled blocks of mossy sandstone cumber the stream below.

'Yo' mun tek along yonder bonky piece till yo' come to th' foredraught, and then foller it all the way; but 'tis a terr'ble weedy road,' says a country lad of whom we ask a direction. So away we go once more, with the blackbirds and thrushes warbling in every hedgerow; until ere long the homely houseroofs of Acton Burnell come in sight, backed by the rolling woodlands of the park, which spreads away in gentle undulations up the slopes of a neighbouring hill.

A pretty, rustic spot is Acton Burnell, its comely thatched cottages, half submerged amidst oldfashioned country flowers, extending crosswise along the lanes, and never an inn to be found in all the place! Yet, despite its present bucolic aspect, Acton Burnell has figured in the annals of English history, as we shall presently see; so let us now go in search of records of those far-away times.

After passing the cosy-looking rectory, with its cedar trees and sweet-smelling lilac, we soon come to the church, a beautiful structure replete with interest to the lover of old-world scenes; for Acton Burnell church was built just at the time when Gothic architecture had attained its high-water mark, and, though of modest dimensions, so perfect is every detail, that the little edifice is worthy of close examination. The annexed sketch shows the fine geometrical east window, and a beautiful three-light window in the north wall of the chancel. The tower, though modern, harmonizes well with the older work beside it, and contains a peal of very sweet-toned bells:

'A nut and a kernel !
Say the Bells of Acton Burnell.'

There is much to be seen in the interior. Near the porch we observe an elegant font, with small, well moulded arches supporting it. Overhead is a good oak roof, though not so massive as that of the chancel. A curious feature of the latter is a small square window low down in the north wall, supposed to be a leper's, or anchorite's, window, as it appears probable that an anchorite had his dwelling here in very early times. Or may not this have been what was known as a 'dead-light,' a little window whence a light was shown into the graveyard to scare away the ghosts !

Passing into the north transept, which has ancient tiles upon the floor, we are at once attracted by the very handsome and well preserved marble monument of a knight clad in rich armour, a ruff around his neck, a lion at his feet, and a quaint little figure supporting a helmet above his head. Near the right hand lies a gauntlet, and within it crouches a diminutive dog, the emblem of fidelity. Alongside the knight reposes his lady consort, her costume of ruff and stomacher, girdle and flat head-dress, bespeaking the time of Queen Elizabeth ; while in the background appear their nine children, habited in the stiff, formal gear of that period. Beneath the enclosing arch are inscribed the words, 'HIC IACET CORPUS RICHARDI LEE ARMIGERI QUI OBIIT 27° DIE MAII ANNO DOÑI 1591.' This fine monument is carved in alabaster, and is surmounted by a knightly helmet and squirrel crest, and coats of arms with supporters.

In the angle of the adjacent wall is another marble tomb, less elaborate than the last, but considerably older. Its arcaded sides are

ACTON -
BURNELL.
H.T.T.

wrought with consummate skill, while the upper surface is inlaid with a handsome brass effigy of Nicholas de Handlo, who in the year 1360 married the heiress, and assumed the name, of the Burnell family. A glance at the sketch will show how well this fine old brass has withstood the wear and tear of more than 500 years. The knight's head is crowned by a peaked hauberk, and the soldierly face, with its long, flowing moustache, looks out from a richly cusped and crocketed canopy. A leather jerkin is worn over the tight-fitting coat of chain-mail, and a jewelled belt supports the long-handled sword and dagger. The legs are encased in greaves; and huge spurs, flexible foot-gear, and gauntlets upon the uplifted hands, complete the tale of this warrior's battle harness. A couchant lion, or griffin, keeps ward beside the feet, and upon a brass plate at the head we read the following inscription:

NICHOLAS DE BURNELL

Hic iacet dn̄s Nichus Burnell miles dn̄s De holgot' qui obiit xix° die Januarii Anno Dni M^{mo} CCC^{mo} Lxxxii° Cui aie ppiciet' ds am.

We have by no means exhausted the attractions of this interesting interior, but, to make a long story short, will merely remark, en passant, there are numerous objects worthy of note in other parts of the church.

A stone's throw distant from the sacred edifice, overshadowed by stately trees, rise the ivy-mantled walls and turrets of Acton Burnell Castle, originally founded by Sir Robert Burnell, sometime chaplain and private secretary to Prince Edward, afterwards King Edward I. It is recorded that in the year 1284 Burnell received the royal license to crenellate his castle at Acton, and the picturesque ruin now before us is a work of that period.

The castle stands four-square, its length from east to west somewhat greater than the width, a slender turret rising at either corner. The moat is conspicuous by its absence, which goes to confirm the theory that Acton Burnell was rather an early embattled mansion, like its neighbour of Stokesay, than a military castle of the usual mediæval type. These massive old ruddy-grey sandstone walls are pierced with mullioned windows, whose vacant cavities still retain fragments of geometrical tracery; while a pathetic-looking wooden turret, in the last stages of decay, peeps out from the mantle of ivy that envelopes the western front. One or two noble old cedar trees, rising close at hand, fling their cool, dappled shadows athwart the level greensward; and beyond them we catch a glimpse of richly timbered park land.

Out there beneath a clump of elms, where the rooks are making merry, certain fragments of grey crumbling stonework are seen, so thither we now bend our steps. These prove to be two lofty massive gables of early Edwardian, or perhaps Norman, date, the last survivals of the hall of the original castle, or manor-house, of Acton Burnell. This secluded spot has become famous from the fact that here, for the first time in history, Lords and Commons sat in council, under the presidency of King Edward I., and proceeded to enact what is known as the 'Statutum de Mercatoribus,' or Statute of Acton Burnell. That took place in the year of grace 1283, just a year before Sir Robert Burnell began the erection of the later mansion, whose ruins we have just visited.

So, before taking leave of the place, we call to mind that when John Leland the antiquary journeyed this way, early in the sixteenth century, he found at Acton Burnell 'a goodly manor Place, or Castel, iiii myles from Shrewsbyri, wher a Parliament was kepte in a greate Barne. It was first made,' he adds, 'by one Burnell, a Byshope.' Robert Burnell, whose name is so closely identified with this his native place, seems to have found favour in the sight of his Sovereign, for Edward I. advanced him to the see of Bath and Wells, and created his faithful liege Lord Treasurer, and Chancellor of the realm. Burnell was frequently employed by the king in affairs of state, especially in connection with the Welsh Marches; and, dying in 1292, was buried in his own cathedral of Wells. His descendants dwelt subsequently at Holgate, in Corve Dale, and the family appears to have finally died out some time in the fifteenth century.

On the brow of a hill two miles away to the eastward stands the diminutive village of Kenley, the birthplace of Sir Archibald Alison, the historian, whose father was incumbent of this parish. The road thither leads past Acton Burnell Hall, a large, white, stone-built mansion, vastly fine with porticoes and pediments, such as our ancestors loved, and seated in a broad, tree-shaded park, very pleasant to behold.

KENLEY CHURCH.

The little church of Kenley is ancient and interesting, having an aisle-less nave, south porch, and broad, low, western tower, with walls thick enough for a fortress, and narrow, deeply-splayed loops by way of windows. The lofty old pulpit, with its sounding-board and curiously carved oak panels, is a pretty feature of the interior; and the chancel window, we notice, is of rather uncommon character, having elegant flowing tracery, and minute sculptured heads outside at the springings of the hoodmould.

Out in the churchyard grows a gnarled old yew tree of immense girth; and from beneath its sombre branches we obtain a glorious prospect over a wide stretch of picturesque, broken country towards the west, with many a familiar Salopian height belted with woods and pastures, and the wild Welsh hills, cloud-capped and blue, rising far away beyond all.

Returning to Acton Burnell, we now put the best foot foremost, and push on again in a southerly direction through a hilly-and-daley country. Just outside the village our attention is arrested by a pair of patriarchal oaks rising close beside the roadway, excellent specimens of the 'Shropshire weed,' which, the rustics will tell you, date from just after the Deluge! Anon we coast beside a belt of woodland all flushed with the shimmery blue of wild hyacinths; and then pause at the crest of the bank for a glance at the distant hills, and the steeples of Salop rising from the vale beneath.

A turn to the left, and yonder is Langley Chapel, standing ruinous and deserted in the midst of a weed-grown meadow, its weatherstained walls and broken roof presenting such a lamentable spectacle of neglect and desecration, that the very genius loci must shed tears, one would suppose, to behold its sorry plight. The exterior is simple, not to say severe, a crazy wooden bellcot above the western gable alone relieving the skyline of the solid old stone-tiled roof, while wooden shutters, all awry, obscure the ancient windows.

Even worse, if possible, is the state of affairs within; for the sacred edifice presents all the appearance of having been used as a cattle stall or sheep pen. Yet amidst all the dust, mildew and litter, a sharp eye may still discover here and there traces of better things. Opposite the door by which we enter rises the old canopied Reader's pew that figures in our sketch, its panelled roof set about with the nests of house-martins, the little denizens twittering to and fro while we sketch. And yonder beneath the broken east window are ranged the desks, tables and benches, just as they were left by the old Puritan worshippers, a curious if not unique feature of the church; while on the opposite side may be noticed some of the original seventeenth-century oak pews, with their bits of finely executed carving, quaint hinges, and nicely turned finial knobs. The date 1601, cut on one of the tiebeams of the roof, gives a clue to the age of the building.

'Scarce a myle from Acton Burnell,' says John Leland, 'standeth Langley Hall, seated very low and flat in a Parke full of woodds, the dwelling place of the Lees, whiche may well challendge to be ranged among the families that are of the better worthe and greater antiquitie in the tract.' Langley Hall is now, alas ! no more, but the Gatehouse seen in our sketch conveys some idea of the appearance it must have

presented. This fine old structure probably dates from about John Leland's time, and, though fallen sadly into disrepair, still delights the eye with its rough, mossy roofs, huge chimney stacks, and ancient, weatherstained gables. A tall pointed archway constructed of stone formed the approach to the original mansion ; and part of an embattled wall that surrounded the demesne does duty nowadays as a cartshed.

Langley was, as we have seen, for many generations the paternal abode of the Lees, a family of much repute in this locality. Richard Lee, whose handsome monument we saw in Acton Burnell church, was a scion of this house, which at a later period claimed some distinguished sons in America, Colonel Richard Lee having emigrated to that country in 1641. General Henry Lee served under Washington, and his son Robert became famous as the leader of the Confederate armies during the Civil War in America.

So much, then, for Langley. Sketches completed, we now shoulder our knapsacks, and push briskly onwards again, dropping into a secluded lane that runs between low, wooded hills, in the direction of the south. Away upon the crest of the ridge to our right stands Frodesley Lodge, a singular looking pile of Tudor brickwork, with a great stone staircase running from top to bottom, and several large oak-panelled chambers. Down in the vale beyond lies Frodesley village, where Sir Herbert Edwardes, the hero of Mûltan, first saw the light, his father being rector of Frodesley at that time. The church was rebuilt in 1809, and is a fair sample of the dismal 'style' then in vogue, about the only relic of antiquity that has survived being the ancient parish register, the oldest in this county, dating from 1598.

A mile or two to the westward lies Longnor, a pretty village with thatched, half-timbered cottages, rising with nonchalant irregularity beside the highway. Longnor Hall, a substantial red-brick structure, stands in the midst of a finely timbered park, in one corner whereof rises the early eighteenth-century chapel, a curious little edifice with the pigeon-hole pews of the 'churchwarden' era, and gates carefully locked lest, perchance, the lover of old things should spy out the nakedness of the land!

But we digress. Upon overhauling the Ordnance sheet, the name 'Devil's Causeway' whets one's curiosity, and puts one upon the qui

Ancient Bridge on the 'Devil's Causeway.

vive for what may lie in store. Nor do we have long to wait, for, coming to a brook in the bottom of the valc, our lane is carried across it by a little round-arched stone bridge, showing unmistakable signs of antiquity. The lane, too, becomes as we proceed a veritable causeway, both it and the ancient bridge being rudely paved with large, thick, roughly squared flagstones, partly hidden beneath grass and weeds, and forming a kind of kerb above the ditch by the laneside.

Tradition has it that this causeway marks the track of an old, old road, that in prehistoric times ran across country from the Watling Street, near Acton Burnell, to the Roman encampment at Nordy Bank, on the shoulder of Brown Clee Hill.

Anent the origin of the bridge itself, an old countrywoman good-naturedly comes to our aid, and solves the riddle by explaining, 'It was the Devil as builded un up in one night, and when cock-crow come er dropped they stwuns down in a hurry out of's apern, and flew away to his own place.'

Thus enlightened we go our ways, and, breasting the hill, come by-and-by to Chatwall, a large, antiquated farmhouse, approached through a sort of cutting in the solid limestone rock. Though ignored by the guidebooks, Chatwall is evidently a place that 'could a tale unfold,' had its old grey stones but tongues wherewith to tell it. The house, a big old structure, solidly built of timber and stone, with rough, stone shingled roof, and low-browed, mullioned windows, was for many a day the home of the Corfields, a family of distinction in these parts, whose initials appear upon the carved oak panelling, with the date 1659. The farm-kitchen inside might have served as a subject for Van Ostade, so rude and primitive it is, with its great oaken settle in the ingle nook, and mighty Jacobean table, inches thick, so constructed as to well-nigh double its length when fully extended.

Through crooked byways, abloom with bluebells and gay pink campion, we now make our way to Church Preen, a tiny hamlet set in a romantic dell, 'far from the madding crowd.' Overshadowed by a gigantic yew, the little church stands as a sort of appendix to Norman Shaw's handsome, half-timbered manor-house, the residence of Mr. Sparrow, the lord of the manor. Dedicated to St. John the Baptist, this church is a singular one, being only about 12 feet wide, though as much as 70 feet in length. It has neither aisles nor transepts, and is of early character, having formerly been used by Cluniac monks as a cell

PANEL AT CHURCH PREEN

or chapel to Wenlock Priory. Though plain and simple to a degree, the interior looks bright and well-cared-for, and boasts a richly carved lectern and pulpit, with the date 1641 cut upon a panel.

Once more afoot, half an hour's walk through shady lanes, with scarce a cottage in sight, leads us past a large, curious-looking old farmhouse at Holt Preen, and so up the hill to Plash.

Seated upon a gentle eminence within its own walled demesne, the Manor-house of Plash is one of the most remarkable and interesting places in all this countryside. The mansion is a large, substantial brick structure, whose tall, twisted chimney stacks, and lofty mullioned windows, indicate that it was built in the days of Henry VIII. or Elizabeth, the low screen wall and ogee cupolas being additions of a later period.

Inside there is a noble sixteenth-century banqueting hall, with open timbered roof, and minstrels' gallery, supported by a massive oak screen of Jacobean character, at one end; and several fine wainscoted apartments with enriched plaster ceilings. An elaborate old fireplace of *cast-iron*, dated 1574, is a noticeable feature. Altogether the old mansion remains pretty much as originally built, affording an interesting study to the antiquary.

The manor of Plash, or Plaish, was held for many generations by the Sprencheaux family, the last of whom, Sir Fulk Sprencheaux, died

in 1447. His portrait, and the armour worn by him, may be seen hanging upon the panelled wall in the banqueting hall at Plash. After them came the Leightons, by one of whom the existing mansion was probably erected; while a later scion of the same stock was a certain William Leighton, whose sumptuous monument we shall presently see when visiting Cardington church.

But the day wanes, and it is still a far cry to our night's bivouac at Church Stretton. So pushing merrily onwards, we call no halt this side of Cardington, our lengthening shadows bringing up the rear, and a cuckoo rehearsing his tedious lay from a solitary wych elm in the hedgerow.

The village lies high on the hills, in an out-of-the-way locality, and very picturesque the old place looks as we draw near, its weatherbeaten grey church crowning a gentle rise, a group of children playing 'hide-and-seek' about the churchyard wicket, and half a dozen antiquated cottages clustering loosely around—rough old stone-built structures most of them, with moss-grown roofs, and diamond-paned windows blinking from beneath the deepset eaves.

But let us step into the church. Entering beneath a seventeenth century timbered porch, its round-arched doorway and the two small

LEIGHTONS OF PLASHE.

Norman lights on either side the nave shew that the fabric is of ancient origin, although its more striking features date from a much later period. The panels of the oak pulpit are effectively carved, while some of the older pews bear the names of local manors, or townships, cut upon them.

In the chancel stands the rich, sumptuous monument of Sir William Leighton and his lady, with their children grouped in a panel of the substructure below. 'THIS MONUMENT WAS MADE,' as the inscription runs, 'IN THE YEAR 1607, AS A MEMORIAL TO WM LEIGHTON OF PLASHE, ESQ., OF NORTH WALES, ONE OF THE COUNCELL IN THE MARCHES OF WALES FOR ABOVE FORTIE YEARES.' Then comes the moral, 'NEMO ANTE OBITUM BEATUS.' A very quaint monument this. Curious, too, are the Bell-ringers' Laws set up on the tower wall.

Bidding farewell to Cardington, we have a good half-mile of collar work before us, ere the brow of the hill is won close to a singular mass of tumbled rocks called the Sharpstones, whence the view opens out towards Wenlock Edge, with Brown Clee peeping over it.

Plunging into a steep stony lane, a likely-looking field path suggests the possibility of a short cut; but, calling to mind the Spaniard's proverb, 'No hay atajo sin trabajo'—no short cut without trouble—we consult an old fellow who happens along just now. 'Yon's a weedy road,' is the best he can say for our byway, 'the medders be all-of-a-pop (boggy) down that-a-way.'

CHALICE AT HOPE BOWDLER.

So we stick to our last, and push forwards again along the stony lane; and half an hour later find ourselves at Hope Bowdler, a lowly hamlet seated in a sheltered vale, in the lap of the Cardington hills. Passing the wheelwright's shop, with its fascinating jumble of rough timber and derelict carts, we turn through the old lich-gate and take a peep at St. Andrew's church, a poorly-restored edifice with a carved oak Jacobean pulpit, and a plain but well-proportioned silver chalice, bearing the date 1572 upon its lid.

Up, up we go once more, with the hills folding in as we advance, and the curious Gaerstone rock sticking up, like a miniature Matterhorn, high above the roadway. Diverging to the right, we soon drop into a sweet secluded 'cwm' beneath the shadow of giant Caradoc, whose rugged crest fairly bristles with huge rocks, as though Titans had been playing bowls up there. Anon we are footing it athwart the open hill-side, pushing through gorse and breast-high bracken, and inhaling the odours of wild thyme and the thousand scents of summer.

Grandly the Longmynd bulks ahead as we descend into Stretton Dale, his massive shoulders rising purple against the amber light that still irradiates the western heavens, while the shadows of evening enfold as with dusky wings each nook and recess of the mountain. The lights of Church Stretton twinkle out through the gloom as we beat up for quarters at last, and a certain snug hostelry to which we now make our way proves a welcome haven after our long day's cross-country tramp.

SIR RALPH DE PITCHFORD.

STRETTON DALE AND THE LONGMYND. A VISIT TO STOKESAY CASTLE.

CHURCH STRETTON is 'a pretty uplandish Townelett, the cheifest Building that is in Stretton Dale.' Thus wrote John Leland in the time of King Henry VIII., and his description holds good to-day. Lovers of Nature will congratulate themselves on the fact that the 'cheifest Building' scarce attains the dignity of a town, which is seated in the midst of one of the most charming localities in all Shropshire, an excellent centre for anyone bent upon exploring the heather-clad hills and upland valleys by which the place is surrounded.

The railway train that carries the traveller thither climbs steadily up-hill all the way from Shrewsbury, halts for breath, so to speak, at Stretton station, and then starts away upon a downward grade, following for many a mile the southward flowing streams. Lying thus high and dry, Church Stretton is one of the healthiest places imaginable, thanks to pure water, and mountain breezes fraught with an invigorating tang from their journey over leagues of gorse, heather and bracken.

Right through the vale, from north to south, runs the ancient green lane still known as Watling Street, rubbing shoulders as it goes with the old winding coach-road, and with that modern parvenu the railway track. For this Stretton valley has time out of mind been the great main artery of travel for man and beast, whether faring towards the cities of the north, or journeying into South Wales.

Church Stretton.

Church Stretton village—or should we say town?—rambles in by no means unpicturesque fashion alongside the old highroad, half way or thereabouts between Shrewsbury and Ludlow. Just off the street, at the rear of the Buck's Head Inn (formerly the manor-house of Church Stretton), stands the parish church of St. Lawrence, a fine cruciform structure shaded by noble old elms, amidst whose green

foliage its venerable grey tower, adorned with the image of the patron saint, rises with charming effect.

The chancel is evidently the work of Norman hands, but an archaic little image, carved above its southern door, looks like an insertion from some earlier edifice. And there are other features well worth looking at in the nicely-proportioned interior; notably a fine thirteenth century roof, some curiously carved oak panelling round about the altar, and groups of heads peering out with odd effect upon the sculptured capitals of the pillars.

Bonham Norton's fine old timbered market house, built in the year 1617, has, unfortunately, been stupidly destroyed not so very long ago—'it was politics as did it' is the dark saying of an old inhabitant; and its place is now usurped by a sorry red-brick substitute of the meanest character. Though the tide of modernization has already set in here, there are still a few ancient timbered gables with lattice-paned windows shewing here and there about the village, and they appear all the more venerable, perhaps, in contrast to their spick-and-span neighbours.

Overlooking Church Stretton upon its western side rise a series of tall, green, rounded hills, outposts of the broad backed Longmynd. In and between these run deep, hollow dingles, or 'gutters,' as they call them hereabouts.

Such is the Carding Mill valley, by which we may climb to the crest of the ridge, whence a shrewd walker may push on to the solitary pole that marks the top of the Longmynd, some 1,700 feet above the sea. If by good fortune the day be clear, the wanderer may reckon on a widespread view from the summit of the Longmynd; tumbled blue hills shewing all around the horizon, like waves on a stormy ocean. An ancient grass-grown trackway traversing these highlands is referred to in old documents as the 'King's hie waie on Longemunde.'

Wayfarers are few on these upland byways, where the hill ponies are often the only signs of life, and no sound breaks the stillness save the whirr of a startled grouse, or the plaintive pipe of the curlew; 'there the winds sweep, and the plovers cry.'

Bright and exhilarating looks the Longmynd in its summer panoply of heather and golden gorse; and picturesque in the extreme when

Autumn brings the 'whimberry' gatherers, with their camp-fires and steaming kettles, and merry shouts of children. But very different is the scene when this vast, unenclosed moorland falls under the stern sway of winter, and every landmark is obliterated by a mantle of untrodden snow. At times like these the Longmynd bears an eerie name, for lives not a few have been lost in attempting to traverse its trackless wastes, and places here and there bear ominous names such as Deadman's Hollow, Devil's Mouth, Deadman's Beach, and the like. Moreover the last fair of the year, held at Church Stretton on St. Andrew's day, has acquired the title of 'Deadman's Fair,' as men returning from it have been known to perish while endeavouring to reach their homes beyond the hills through the wild, mid-winter night. A remarkable if not unprecedented experience was that which befell the Rev. Donald Carr, the present rector of Woolstaston, who was lost in the snow upon Longmynd for a night and a day, in January, 1865.

* * * * * *

Extending our rambles somewhat farther afield, a few minutes' run by train beneath the steep, wooded slopes of Caer Caradoc, brings us to

Leebotwood, the first station Shrewsbury-wards on the railway. The village itself lies a quarter of a mile away, under a smooth green hill called the Lawley, but is worth a détour for the sake of its pretty thatched cottages, with their flowery garden plots and wealth of creepers, and its quaint oldfashioned inn yclept The Pound, which bears the date 1650, and does duty also as village post-office.

WOOLSTASTON CHURCH, AND RECTORY.

Past Leebotwood church, a small stone edifice overarched by umbrageous beech trees, we push on along the dusty highway, which, gradually ascending, affords fine views over the country-side, and a glimpse of a round green 'tump' called Castle Hill, a prehistoric camp keeping ward over the ancient Portway, which extends hence along the brow of the Longmynd to Billing's Ring, near Bishop's Castle.

A turn of the road reveals the village of Woolstaston, with its diminutive church overshadowed by three gigantic yew trees, and snug timbered rectory house, home of the Rev. Donald Carr, whose marvellous adventures, when snowed up on the Longmynd, have been recorded in an interesting little work entitled 'A Night in the Snow;' adventures which seem to confirm the old adage that 'truth is stranger than fiction.'

Woolstaston church, despite its small size, is well worth a passing visit. The chancel is entered through a doorway of true pre-Norman type, its semicircular head being fashioned from one single stone, while the jambs retain the holes for a wooden cross-bar. But the most notable feature of the church is a singular pair of fonts, one standing within the other, as depicted in our sketch. Both are evidently very ancient, and of archaic simplicity, the lower and seemingly older one

FONT AT WOOLSTASTON.

being supposed to have originally belonged to a chapel, long since destroyed, that stood not far from here.

Woolstaston Hall, now a large farmhouse, stands near the church. It must have been a fine place in its time, if we may judge from a noble panelled parlour, with a polished oak floor fit to make young people's feet itch for a dance, and a massive stone portal, fronting upon the garden to the rear, evidently the main entrance to the mansion in its original state.

In the secluded country to the north of Woolstaston one stumbles upon a bunch of out-of-the-way villages and hamlets, anent which runs the following quatrain:

> 'Cothercot upo' the Hill,
> Wilderley down i' the Dale,
> Churton for pretty Girls,
> And Powtherbatch for good Ale!'

In the same quarter lies Beatchcott, a place boasting a history of its own, having been granted by Henry III. to Haughmond Abbey, an oratory being in existence here at that time. Beatchcott subsequently passed to the Ireland family, coming eventually into the possession of the Wildings, who have held the estate for over three hundred years.

At Ratlinghope, a few miles away, the Black Canons of St. Augustine had a small cell, or priory, founded in John's reign, and affiliated to Wigmore Abbey.

Returning from Woolstaston to Church Stretton, we pass by Womerton, where the older of the two fonts in Woolstaston church was found; and then, skirting the unenclosed uplands, we drop into the highroad at or about All Stretton.

Anent these names of Stretton hangs a tale that runs somewhat as follows. King Charles II. (or was it James?), journeying one day towards Shrewsbury, came in due course to Little Stretton. 'How call you this place?' inquired the Merrie Monarch. 'Stretton, an it please your Majesty,' was the countryman's reply. '*Little* Stretton, methinks, were a fitter name for so small a place,' said the King; and set forth again towards Shrewsbury. Upon arriving at the next village, Charles again asked where he was. 'At Stretton, sire,' someone answered. Espying the parish church, whose bells were making music in the old grey steeple, his Majesty exclaimed: 'Call it rather *Church* Stretton,' and went his way once more. Finally the King came to All Stretton, and being again informed he was at Stretton, 'Stretton!' cried Charles in astonishment, 'why it's *All* Stretton about here!' The story, if not absolutely true, is at least 'ben trovato.'

* * * * * *

The road from Church Stretton to Craven Arms traverses a pleasant, smiling vale, with the Quenny brook wimpling along amidst water meadows, and broad breezy hillslopes stretching up and away beyond the rich, rolling woodlands that nestle around their flanks.

A short mile out of the village we strike up an isolated knoll, whose summit is seamed with the green ramparts of Brockhurst Castle, an ancient stronghold keeping ward over the Watling Street, of whose history very little is known. Brockhurst was a royal foundation, and in Henry the Second's reign was held by Engelard de Pitchford, the famous Hubert de Burgh being Castellan in the year 1226. As early as Queen Elizabeth's time the place, it is evident, was already deserted; for Camden, writing at that period, finds there 'are still remaining the ruins of an ancient castle, called Brocard's castle, surrounded by verdant meads which anciently were fishponds.' But the site is an ideal spot for the genus picnicker, by whom its bowery nooks and secluded, fern-clad dingles are often-times frequented.

On descending to the highroad, we notice the level strath where doubtless the fishponds lay. Soon afterwards we come to Little Stretton, a tranquil hamlet charmingly located in a nook of the Longmynd, over against the beautifully-wooded hill of Ragleth. The cottagers, we observe, take a curious delight in garnishing their doorways with derelict cannon-shot, which they find in the neighbouring gullies after artillery practice on the Longmynd. Blackleaded and brightly polished, they stand sentinel on either side the rustic porch; an innocent billet indeed for these truculent bullets!

At the farther end of the village two humble inns, the Green Dragon and the Crown, stand vis-à-vis on either side the highway; and, in these modest hostelries, visitors may possibly identify the rival 'houses' that figure in Beatrice Harraden's story of Shropshire life, entitled 'At the Green Dragon.'

Pushing on now to Marsh Brook, we turn sharp to the left at the rural post-office, and work our way up-hill to Acton Scott, a high-lying place some 700 feet above sea level—'Acton-super-Montem' it is called in ancient documents.

Passing through the churchyard wicket, we pause beneath an enormous hollow yew tree to scan the rare prospect over the rolling Stretton hills, and a glimpse down the vale towards Ludlow. Of the church itself there is little to be said, save that it has a good plain old oak roodscreen ; so we stroll on beneath an avenue of noble beech trees, and presently come in sight of Acton Scott Hall.

As may be seen in our sketch, the mansion is a simple, massive brick structure, with stone quoins at the angles, mullioned windows, and clustered chimney shafts ; altogether a very fair specimen of an ancestral abode of the gentlefolk of a bygone period. And the place has an added interest for all local antiquaries, as the home of the late Mrs. Stackhouse-Acton, author of 'Castles and Mansions of Shropshire.' Acton Scott Hall was in all probability erected by a certain Edward Acton, who flourished about the middle of the sixteenth century ; and it has been noticed that the mansion bears a considerable resemblance to its contemporary, the so-called 'Whitehall' at Shrewsbury.

A steep 'pitchy' lane, descending the hill past the cosy-looking vicarage, now leads us across a stretch of rough common-land, where the cottagers' geese seem disposed, more suo, to contest our right-of-way. Thence by narrow lanes draped with ferns and wild flowers we travel on to a place called Alceston, and at an elbow of the road come face-to-face with the old derelict homestead that figures below; its weather-stained roofs tufted with green mosses and houseleeks, and overshadowed by a few ragged fir trees; while the black old timbers upon its faded front are wrought into balusters and quatrefoil patterns.

In its palmy days Alceston seems to have been a place of some consequence, having been built by Humphrey Hill (a connection of the Hills of Court-of-Hill), who died here in 1585. The house was originally much larger, great part of it having been pulled down many years ago.

Over against this ancient dwelling rises a very large and happily quite unrestored old barn, entirely constructed of oak both inside and out; a pleasing contrast to those modern monstrosities of galvanized iron, that too often stare one out of countenance amidst these rural byways.

Through a pleasant, well-tended country, relieved by scraps of common-land, we win our way to Wistanstow, a comely-looking village extending along a quiet road, on the line of the ancient Watling Street.

Close beside the highway rises the old grey tower of its parish church, a fine cruciform structure dating from 1180, A.D. Upon the nail-studded south nave door hangs a so-called 'sanctuary' ring, and the great wooden lock with its iron letters I.P.C.W., and date 1696. The walls of the south transept bear well-executed writings of the Creed, the Lord's Prayer and the Decalogue, of early seventeenth century date; while the north transept retains its old original oak roof. The chancel door shews the characteristic round arch and quaintly-carved capitals of the Norman style.

We have now but to steer a straight course for awhile, as the Watling Street fares forward between its trim, green hedgerows. But anon we go astray once more in order to get a nearer look at Halford church, which peeps invitingly out from a leafy nook on the opposite

bank of the Onny. The little church, though considerably modernized, bears traces of no mean antiquity, and with an old flour-mill down in the vale below is reflected in the stream at our feet, affording as pretty a coup d'œil as anyone could wish to see.

So having 'bagged' a sketch of this pleasant scene we take it easy awhile, lying prone amidst the clover-scented grass and the buttercups under the shade of an old pollard willow, and watching the troutlets as they rise at the silly gnats, and the swallows flashing by in the sunlight. Then, giving Craven Arms village the go-by for the present, we tramp the dusty half-mile of highroad that leads to Stokesay Castle.

STOKESAY CASTLE SHROPSHIRE.

Presently the old grey-green walls and mossy roofs of castle and church come into view beyond a clump of trees upon our right, arousing great expectations of matters antiquarian; for, as Dr. Jessop truly remarks, 'when a man is bitten with a taste for old castles and earthworks, it is all over with him.'

Half fortalice, half manor-house, Stokesay Castle rears its ancient turrets in the midst of a green, sylvan vale, the luxuriantly wooded heights that rise on either hand giving a sense of restful seclusion; while one or two farmsteads, nestling beneath the old ivy-mantled walls, lend a home-like air to this pleasant, rural scene.

Making our way around to its south-western side, we obtain what is, perhaps, the best general view of the castle; its hoary towers and gables appearing from this point mirrored in the placid surface of a large pool, which in olden times supplied water to the moat.

The venerable structure that now rises so picturesquely before us is regarded by antiquaries as an almost unique example of a thirteenth-century mansion which has been fortified at some period subsequent to the erection of the domestic portion of the buildings, thus reversing the usual order of things.

Hence the tall crenellated tower that figures conspicuously in our sketch is not, as would at first sight appear, the oldest part of the castle, but was built at a later period in order to protect John de Verdon's already existing mansion, whose mossy gables and tall mullioned windows are seen farther away to the left. The curious-looking bastion beyond, with its quaint, overhanging upper story, is a remarkable feature of the edifice; its lower portion, pierced with loops for archery, being probably older than any other part of the castle, though the half-timbered gable above is a comparatively modern addition.

In the background rises the low grey tower of the parish church, an interesting old edifice untouched as yet by restoration, whereof we shall see more anon.

We now proceed to the Gatehouse, a beautiful structure of timber and plaster dating from Tudor times. Grey, worn, and weather-stained as they are, its solid old oaken timbers bid fair to outlast many a long year yet ; while the huge angle corbels and the spandrils above the gateway are boldly carved with the quaint, humorous conceits of the mediæval craftsman. The story goes that in the last century this

THE GATE-HOUSE, STOKESAY CASTLE.

Gatehouse used to be frequented by a fugitive, outlawed in the days when forgery was a capital crime, who hid snugly away in some secret closet of the interior until the hue-and-cry was well on its way elsewhere.

Let us now make our way within. A substantial oak door, nail-studded, and loopholed for the use of muskets, admits us into the courtyard; beyond whose level greensward rise the picturesque gables of the ancient Banqueting Hall, its mullioned windows flanked by massive buttresses, and surmounted with a wavy old stone-slated roof beautified by lush green mosses and splashes of golden lichen.

Passing within, we find ourselves in a nobly proportioned hall, whose open-timbered roof is supported by sturdy oaken beams springing from stone corbels of elegant design. Upon either side rise lofty traceried windows; and in the floor we see the stone slab which supported the brazier, whose smoke has blackened the rafters overhead.

At one end of the hall a rude sort of staircase, composed of solid oak steps, gives access to other rooms in the northern wing of the castle; and in the opposite wall is a shouldered doorway, leading to storerooms and nondescript cellars. High up in this wall are seen two tiny, shuttered lights, which give upon the Banqueting Hall from an upper chamber.

To this apartment, known as the Solar, we now make our way; climbing thither by a flight of stone steps out in the open courtyard. With its magnificent carved oak mantelpiece and handsome wainscoting, the Solar must have been far and away the most sumptuous chamber in the castle, and was probably used as a kind of parlour, or withdrawing-room, for ladies, and guests of the better sort. This view is strengthened by the presence of the two 'peep-hole' windows before mentioned, whence the occupants of the Solar could, themselves unobserved, keep an eye upon the festive scenes that went forward in the Banqueting Hall below.

The mantelpiece above mentioned is quite a marvel of elaborate ornamentation, of that rich, florid style, in vogue towards the close of the seventeenth century. The base of the structure, surmounting a plain stone fireplace, is effectively carved with bold, conventional foliage, and a pear pattern in the spandrils; while the upper portion is divided pilaster-wise, by grotesque figures, into panels enriched with masks surrounded by intricate strapwork. A sketch of one of these panels may be seen by turning to p. 59, where it forms a tailplate to the chapter.

Both wainscoting and chimney-piece retain remnants of colour and gilding; and the chamber is lighted by traceried windows bearing a general resemblance to those of the adjoining hall.

Old records tell of historical portraits at 'Stoke,' as it was then called; and we can well imagine they adorned the walls of this very apartment. Here was 'ye Picture of Charles ye Fyrst'; there, 'ye Picture of Charles ye Seconde'; and yonder, 'Theodoric Vernon, alias Vernon with ye redde Hand, alias the Proud Vernon, with a gold Chaine about hys neck with a Medall at the bottom.' What with its panelled dadoes, handsome chimney-piece, old portraits looking down from the walls, and armorial quarterings in its stained-glass windows, the Solar must have afforded a seductive retreat from the amenities of those rough times.

A climb to the summit of the great tower is rewarded by a capital coup d'œil of the castle and its pleasant environs; so now, before taking leave of this interesting spot, let us travel back for a moment into the domain of history.

In the Conqueror's time 'Stoke' was held by the famous Roger de Montgomery, passing subsequently to the de Lacys, until it was bestowed by Walter of that ilk on the family of Say, whose ancestors had fought by Duke William's side at the Battle of Hastings. Having reverted to the de Lacys, the last of that line bestowed the castle upon his son-in-law, John de Verdon, who about 1240 A.D. erected the present Banqueting Hall.

Half-a-century later, we find a certain Lawrence de Ludlow obtaining permission to 'crenellate his Castle at Stoke-Say,' at which time the courtyard wall, and possibly the southern tower, may have been erected. John Leland, passing this way on his 'Laborieuse Searche for England's Antiquities,' tells us, with scant regard for topographical accuracy, that 'Mr. Vernon hath a place not farre from Oney, aboot iiij miles out of Ludlo, in the waye betwixt Ludlo and Bishop Castle. Stoke-Say belongeth sometime to the Ludlo's, now the

Vernons, builded like a Castell.' These were the Vernons of Haddon Hall fame, from whom Stokesay passed by purchase to the Earls of Craven.

During the Civil Wars the castle was held by Sir Samuel Baldwyn, of Elsich, and was garrisoned for King Charles; but after a short investment fell into the hands of the Parliamentarians, who defeated and routed a troop of Royalists, 200 strong, close to a place called Whettleton, in the meadows below Norton Camp, on the eastern side

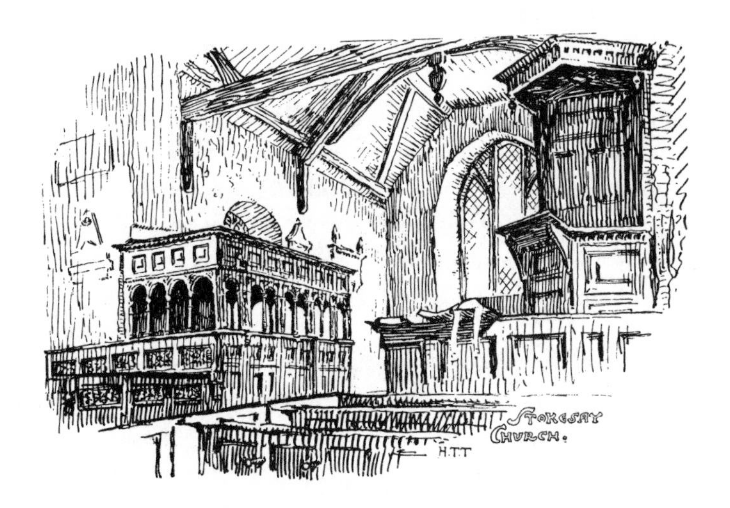

of the vale. Thereafter the castle was 'slighted,' or rendered incapable of defence.

Stokesay Castle is now the property of H. J. Allcroft, Esq., by whom the old place has been put into a reasonable state of repair, and its ancient features carefully preserved. Those who care to know more about this interesting fortified Manor-house, may obtain at the Gatehouse an excellent little guidebook to Stokesay Castle by the Rev. J. D. la Touche, the late vicar of Stokesay.

Stokesay Church, though originally Norman, was in large measure rebuilt in the seventeenth century, as recorded upon the keystone of the tower arch, 'Ano. Dom. 1654, this church was rebuilt by the pious oversight of George Powell, Gent., and George Lambe, Churchwarden. This Arch was given by John Cheshire, Joyner.' A tiebeam of the chancel roof bears a date of ten years later.

Since those times the sacred edifice has remained practically untouched, and consequently presents an appearance of rural simplicity, very grateful to look upon in these 'restoration' days. The oak pulpit, with its curious sounding-board above, and the beautiful double canopied pew in the chancel, are excellent examples of Jacobean carpentry; while some of the old high-backed pews retain their original wrought-iron hinges, and touches of carved work here and there.

Recent researches have revealed, beneath the whitewash of the 'churchwarden' era, certain scriptural texts upon the walls, whose quaint, appropriate sentiment will not be lost upon the beholder. Alongside the pulpit, for example, runs the legend, 'As new born Babes desire ye Sincere milk of ye Word, that ye may grow thereby.' There, too, is the Credence, with the name 'Ponce Pilate,' after the olden fashion.

A primitive west gallery partially obscures the well-proportioned Early English arch opening into the tower, which latter is broad, low and massive, and part of the original church. Outside are some very fair seventeenth-century table tombs, one of them having its fluted pillars scooped away in an unaccountable manner.

Before retracing our steps towards Craven Arms, we strike up into the woods above Whettleton, in order to visit Norton Camp, an early British earthwork altered and adapted, as is supposed, by the Romans, which commands both the ancient Watling Street, and the Castle road going into Corve Dale. Its mounds are large and lofty, especially upon the western side, where the hill falls steeply to the plain, and we obtain glimpses through the twinkling foliage of far-away heights, extending fold upon fold to the horizon. Yonder rise the wild hills of Wales, their purple crests shewing clear and sharp against the glowing sunset sky; while the full moon climbs above the sombre woodlands of Corve Dale, and beams adieu to the departing lord of day.

Then we plunge down through the twilight woods, and, traversing an ancient suburb paradoxically called Newton, with its fine old half-timbered mansion house, once the vicarage of Stokesay, come soon to Craven Arms, where we take up our night's lodging in one of the comfortable hotels for which the place is noted.

CARVED PANEL AT STOKESAY CASTLE

FROM CRAVEN ARMS TO BISHOP'S CASTLE AND CLUN.

OUR general objective to-day is the broken, picturesque country lying around the quiet market towns of Bishop's Castle and Clun; an out-of-the-way, rural district, less frequented, perhaps, than any other portion of Shropshire. The Bishop's Castle railway, commencing at Craven Arms, affords the readiest means of approach to the locality. Away to the south as we jaunt leisurely along we get a glimpse of Cheney Longville, a pretty secluded hamlet hidden away amidst copses and pasture fields, with never a highroad near it. Some slight remains of the old fortified manor-house of Cheney Longville still exist, incorporated with an antiquated farmhouse containing much fine carved oak furniture.

The Cheney family, whence the place derives its name, is a very ancient clan. Roger Cheney was Seneschal to Edward, Earl of Arundel, Sheriff of Shropshire in 1316. A second Roger held 'Cheney Longfield' in 1341; while yet another of the same name received license from the King, 1395 A.D., to embattle his house at Cheney Longville.

After a while we join company with the little river Onny, as it meanders through a picturesquely wooded vale, getting delightful glimpses of the Longmynd as we draw near to our destination, his lower flanks dotted with old stunty oaks and ancient hawthorns, while gorse and heather brighten the foreground.

Coming to Plowden station, we shoulder the knapsacks and bear away to the southward.

Plowden Hall
Shropshire.

Crossing the Onny beside a rushing weir, we get a direction for Plowden Hall from an old fellow in charge of a timber-waggon. 'You'm better tek up the rack acrass yon bonky piece, and goo through the wicket,' says our friend, 'you'll be apt to find it a gainer road than the one as goes through the 'ood.' So we breast the upland meadows, and meanwhile our gaze wanders over a goodly prospect; hill and vale, chequered by tilth and pasture-land, lying map-like at our feet, while shafts of sunlight, touching here and there, relieve the contours of a broken, wrinkled country, or bring into momentary prominence some rustic homestead surrounded by barns and haystacks.

Plowden Hall lies perdu until we are close upon it, for the old mansion nestles in a nook of the hills amidst dark, umbrageous woodlands. Its broad, somewhat low entrance front is pleasantly quaint and simple, with nothing imposing about it, though the deep-browed portico and massive hall door beneath lend a touch of character. But a better view is obtained by passing to the back of the house, whence our sketch is taken.

From this point of view the ancient Manor-house rears its yellow weatherstained gables, slender chimneys and mossy roofs, against the rich dark foliage that clothes the rearward hill; while the close-cropped lawns, the trim yew hedges, and gay-coloured parterres of the old-fashioned garden in the foreground, form an appropriate setting for this beau-ideal of an old English homestead.

Within the mansion one finds a congeries of wainscoted and panelled chambers, whose walls are hung with ancient tapestry, and adorned by ancestral portraits of the Plowden family. Here is Edmund Plowden, the eminent lawyer, who was 'accounted the oracle of the law,' and with whose memory is associated the saying, 'The case is altered; no priest, no mass; no mass, no violation of the law'; a saying which in course of time passed into a common proverb. On the death of his father in 1557, Edmund Plowden succeeded to the estates, and began the building of the present Hall. He was treasurer of the Hon. Society of the Middle Temple, in whose church he lies buried; and might have been Lord Chancellor under

Queen Elizabeth, had he chosen to renounce the ancient Faith of his fathers.

The hall, with its carved oak chimney-piece and quaint Dutch tiles, its panelled walls and oaken floors, has a sombre, dignified air about it. In one wing of the old house is the private chapel, dedicated to St. Francis of Assisi, with a portrait of the patron saint attributed to Michelangelo. Set into the wall of this chapel is a curious old brass, representing Humphrey Plowden and his seven daughters, which was brought hither years ago from Bishop's Castle church. In an adjacent corner a sliding panel gives access to a secret passage-way, by which, in the Reformation days, the officiating priest might at a moment's notice effect his escape from the mansion. The whole place, indeed, is honeycombed from cellar to roof with hidie-holes, closets and secret passages, turning and twisting amidst hatchways and bulkheads, or terminating in breakneck ladders. One of these queer gangways is said to lead out to a lonely spot amidst the woods known as the Lady's Chair; and it goes without saying that the old house has earned the reputation of being haunted.

One would suppose the builders of Plowden Hall had had in their minds the Spaniards' proverb: 'The rat that has only one hole is easily caught.'

The Plowden family can trace, it is said, an unbroken lineage from Roger de Plowden, the Crusader, down to Edmund of that ilk, who died no longer ago than 1838, nearly 700 years. This Roger distinguished himself at the siege of Acre, in 1191; and, upon being taken prisoner by the enemy, made a vow that, if ever he returned in safety to his Shropshire home, he would build a chapel by way of thank-offering; and, as we shall see by-and-by at Lydbury North, the pious knight was as good as his word.

From Edmund Plowden the estate passed to his nephew William, whose son, W. F. Plowden, Esq., is the present owner of the property.

Farewell now to Plowden. Our onward way leads beneath a green avenue of oaks and beeches, whose branches, meeting overhead, cast a dappled shade athwart the lane, and afford a playground for squirrels, woodpeckers, and many another of Nature's children.

Turning our backs upon the low hill where Billing's Ring keeps ward over the ancient Portway, we skirt the shoulder of Oakeley Mynd, Walcot Park with its big red-brick mansion and hanging woods shewing right ahead, with a dark clump of trees cutting against the skyline. Yonder lie Bury Ditches, a fine old British camp whose lofty crest forms a conspicuous landmark for many a mile around.

Avoiding a lot of odd turnings we continue to hug the highroad, which, trending now in a due westerly direction, introduces us to a pleasant, open vale, with the tower of Lydbury church peeping out from a grove of trees in the middle of the village.

Lydbury North is an ancient place, claiming some consideration. In Norman days the episcopal manor of Lydbury formed an important appanage to the Bishopric of Hereford, and the martial prelates of that period had a great stronghold in the vicinity, which, though long since dismantled and demolished, has given its name to the neighbouring town of Bishop's Castle.

But Lydbury church, having remained virtually unaltered by restoration, is one of the most interesting edifices of its kind in all Shropshire. It has a nave and chancel, with north and south chapels, a timbered porch, and broad, massive tower at the western end.

The primitive old clock upon the tower vaguely points the time with a solitary hand, and the roofs of the church are still covered with their original stone slabs, greatly enhancing the picturesque appearance of the ancient building. The solid nail-studded porch door bears traces of bullet marks, and has a pair of fifteenth-century hinges.

The interior of the church wears an antiquated air, as of primæval repose, and appears to belong mainly to the twelfth and thirteenth centuries. Many of the high-backed Jacobean pews are rudely adorned with carving, as is also the oaken pulpit; while one or two of the former still have the link and staple, used in the 'good old times' when the worshippers were accustomed to lock themselves up in their pews, a habit that affords a curious insight into the everyday manners of a bygone generation.

The font looks very primitive and ancient. A good fifteenth-century oak roodscreen divides nave from chancel, and above it appears the Decalogue, finely written in old English lettering of the date 1615. The block of masonry projecting from an adjacent wall was probably a 'penance stone.'

Above the altar are seen two small stone brackets supporting a pair of gilded wooden candlesticks, which, according to local tradition, Archbishop Laud caused to be put there, in place of certain images that had stood upon them before.

A stone tablet upon the north wall of the chancel is interesting in that it records the services of the Rev. J. Ambler, who, after being ousted from this living by the Covenanters, was reinstated at the Restoration.

North and south of the nave open out two chapels, or short transepts, called respectively the Plowden Chapel, and the Walcot Chapel. The Walcots of Walcot are a family of very ancient descent, who have held estates in this locality from time immemorial. After their day, the manor of Walcot passed to the ancestors of Lord Powis, and eventually came into the possession of no less a personage than Robert Clive, Baron Plassey, K.B., founder of the British dominion in India, who died at Walcot Hall in 1774. His name may be seen inscribed in some prayer-books still preserved in this chapel. Upon the wall above the family pew hangs the Walcot escutcheon, with three black pawns, or rooks, amidst its quarterings.

This is explained by the following note in a pedigree of the Walcot family, compiled in 1643, referring to a certain John Walcot who lived in the early part of the fifteenth century. 'This John Walcote, plainge at the Chese with King Henry the fift, Kinge of England, gave hym the check-matte with the Rouke; whereupon the Kinge chainged hys coate of armes, which was the crosse with flower-de-luces, and gave hym the Rouke for a remembrance thereof, by which he and hys posteritie hath continued to this daye.'

The Plowden chapel is separated from the nave by a plain oak screen. As already mentioned, this chapel was built by an ancestor of the Plowdens, after returning in safety from captivity in Asia Minor. It is lighted by several well-proportioned windows of early character, and contains a much dilapidated stone altar of pre-Reformation date, with two brackets up above it, probably intended for images.

In one corner stands a curious sort of grille, or iron railed structure, bearing traces of colour, and surmounted at one end by a gilded iron cross. It was customary, we understand, to place this railing around a newly made grave, to protect it from evil disposed persons.

The tower walls are enormously thick, as though intended to withstand attack. The fine old panelled oak nave roof is now hidden from below by an ugly whitewashed ceiling. The bell-frame up in the belfry is something of a curiosity, being rudely but effectively carved with dragon-like monsters having foliated tails.

We now make for the village inn, with appetites sharp-set for such rustic fare as the place may haply afford. Half-an-hour later finds us climbing the ascent of Oakeley Mynd, with a fresh westerly breeze humming through the tree-tops, and the cloud shadows chasing one another athwart the genial landscape.

Instead of going direct to Bishop's Castle, we steer a due northerly course towards a place named Lea. By so doing we not only avoid a spell of hard highroad, but get into the bargain a rare outlook across a hilly-and-daley country, with a wisp of blue smoke trailing away upon the breeze far off on the shoulder of Longmynd. From the top of the bank, a thousand feet above sea-level, we look across a pleasant vale, where the brown roofs of Bishop's Castle are seen nestling beneath tumbled hills, outliers of Clun Forest.

Then away we go down a rough footpath, or 'rack,' as they call it hereabouts; making a bee-line for our destination, and skirting the head of a deep wooded dingle known as Narrow Dale. Guided by the cheerful barking of dogs, we presently come in sight of a lonely farmstead; and, upon stepping round to the rear, descry a group of buildings all jumbled up together in the manner shewn over page.

'The remains we see,' writes Mr. W. Phillips in 'Shropshire Notes and Queries,' 'are probably the walls of the old square keep. They are built of the Wenlock limestone found in the neighbourhood, and are so well constructed that the lime is harder than the stone, so that, when an attempt was made some years ago to utilize the material, it was found to be less trouble to obtain fresh stones from the quarry. We owe it to this fact that these ruins remain to awaken our curiosity.'

LEA CASTLE.

The walls of this old keep are extremely massive, and have several window and door openings in them of various dates from the fourteenth century onwards. So much has been destroyed that the original dimensions of the castle cannot now be ascertained; but the moat may still in part be traced, besides evidences of fishponds near the little rivulet that filled them.

The Manor of Lea formed, in early days, the largest feudal Lordship in Shropshire held by the Bishop of Hereford. Owing to the exigences of his position, and the turbulence of those remote times, the Bishop was often called upon to relinquish the crozier for the sword, and to lead his lieges against the wild Welshmen; for, in connexion with Bishop's Castle, Lea formed an important link in the cordon of border fortresses. The tenant of Lea, indeed, appears to have been under obligation of doing suit and service at Bishop's Castle, when called upon by the constable of the latter.

The old farmhouse alongside has evidently been added to and altered at various times in a very haphazard fashion. On its staircase is a piece of timber quartering ornamented with a rude shield on which appear the words ANNO. DO. 1560, proving that the place can boast a respectable antiquity.

Amidst a chorus of 'come-back! come-back!' from the galeney-fowls in the farmyard, we set out once again upon our travels. Giving preference to the meadow paths, we presently happen upon a huge block of stone, as big as a good-sized cart, lying stranded in the middle of a grass field. How it came there is the puzzle, so we take counsel with an old fellow breaking stones by the wayside, a furlong farther on. 'Oh,' says he, in reply to our questions, 'they 'ud used to tell us, when we was childern, as the Devil fell lame one day a-walkin' by here, and throwed that there old stwun out of's shoe, and then fled away up to Stiperstones yander. But that was afore my time, like, and behappen there's never a one now as can tell the rights on it.' And the country folk have a saying that the Lea Stone, as it is called, turns itself around 'every time the clock strikes thirteen.'

With the shadows lengthening around we draw near to Bishop's Castle, a place half town, half village, seated upon a southward sloping hill. It was always called Lydbury Castle in the olden days, on account of the castle of that name (built by the Bishops of Hereford to protect their episcopal manor of Lydbury), which stood in a commanding position at the top of the town.

When Henry II. mounted the throne, Bishop's Castle was held by Hugh de Mortimer of Wigmore, but was regained for the see by the energy of Bishop Gilbert Ffoliot. In the year 1263, the castle was stormed and its constable slain by the rebellious John FitzAlan and his followers. A visitation of Bishop Swinfield, about thirty years later, was long remembered in the locality, on account of the sumptuous style in which that prelate lived; indeed his Lordship and his retinue seem to have 'eaten the good people out of house and home,' as the saying goes.

Bishop's Castle is nowadays but a drowsy little market town, yet proud withal of being the metropolis of an extensive agricultural district, and renowned for its great cattle fairs, frequented by breeders and 'men whose talk is of bullocks,' who are attracted hither by the fine race of cattle for which this locality is noted. Then, on May 1, has it not its 'Mop,' or Hiring Fair, when the farm hands and servant girls 'break the year,' as the phrase goes; and you may overhear one goodwife complaining to another, anent some errant handmaid, ''Er's broke 'er 'ear this marnin', I'm afeared 'er'll allus be a rollin' stwun as'll never gether no moss!'

BISHOPS CASTLE
FROM AN OLD PRINT.

In bygone times Bishop's Castle was (and for aught we know is still) ruled by a Mayor and Corporation, with fifteen Aldermen or Capital Burgesses, a Bailiff, and a Recorder. So early as 1572 the town received its first charter from the Sovereign, which was ratified by Charles I. in 1648.

At the very top of the town, where the old coach roads from Wales converge, stands the Castle Hotel, one of those large, roomy caravansarys, frequented by wayfaring men in the days before railways had come to rob the country roads of their cheerful tide of traffic. To the rear of this inn lies an oldfashioned bowling-green, whose area marks the site of the keep-tower of the erstwhile Castle of Lydbury, built to protect the episcopal demesne against the freebooters of the Welsh border.

In Leland's time the Castle was 'well maintenid, and set on a stronge Rokke, not very hi,' but seems to have been already reduced to ruins before the time of the Civil Wars.

Perched on a tall green mound, high above the old town, the position is certainly a commanding one, affording a fine prospect over

the adjacent country, though now somewhat obscured by trees. Close at hand rises the old Market House, now the Powis Institute and Reading Room, with the borough arms carved upon its gable, and the date of its erection, 1781. Over the door of an adjacent shop we espy the curious surname of Gotobed, a clan which should be widely represented, one would suppose, in this Sleepy Hollow! Another old lintel retains some ancient lettering, with the figures 1685. Then, turning down the steep High Street, we get a backward view of the town; the prim façade of an eighteenth-century Town Hall, topped by a slender belfry, seeming to block up the roadway, and some old-fashioned shops and dwellings flanking the narrow footpath.

Presently we come to the church at the farther end of the town, though tradition avers that, once upon a time, the church stood in the very middle of it; not that the church has moved, but the town shrunk up into itself—but that is as it may be. An ancient ivyclad tower is about the only relic of the older church which has survived, for, during the troubles of the Civil Wars, the sacred edifice fell a prey to the flames, and has only within the last forty years been rebuilt and renovated. There are some very ancient yews in the churchyard; and a tombstone near the belfry door bears the following inscription: 'A la mémoire de Louis Paces, Lieut.-Colonel de Chevaux legers, chevalier des ordres militaires des deux Siciles et d'Espayne. Mort à Bishop's Castle le 1re Mai 1814, age de 40 ans.' This must have been one of the French prisoners who, at the time of the Peninsular War, were billeted at Bishop's Castle.

Bishop's Castle forms a good starting-point for exploring a little-frequented, rural country. Northwards lie Lydham and More, Lydham church standing, as is so frequently the case in this border district, cheek-by-jowl with a prehistoric tumulus. More is the ancestral home of the ancient family of that ilk, whose forbears 'came over from Normandy with the Conqueror.'

Then there is Linley, with its stately avenues leading up towards hills which have been mined for lead ever since the Romans were there. Amongst these hills stands Hyssington, which we will take leave to visit, though it lies away outside our county, over the Welsh frontier.

Anent the church at Hyssington there is a curious tradition. Long, long ago, in the old Popish days, an enormous Bull made his appearance at Hyssington, and grew bigger and bigger every day, until the good people of the neighbourhood went in fear of their lives by reason of the dreaded monster. At last things came to such a pass that the parson made up his mind to try heroic measures. So with book, bell and candle, he sallied forth in quest of the Bull, and, by reading of appropriate texts, managed to reduce the uncanny beast to such dimensions as would admit of his being driven into the church. But alack! before the creature could be finally extinguished, parson's candle had burnt out; and ere morning came, when the reading could be resumed, the Bull had swelled out again, until his huge body cracked the church walls from top to bottom!

Such is the veracious legend; but whether this Bull hailed from the Emerald Isle, or belonged to that species known as Papal Bulls, history recordeth not; but the cracks in the church walls long remained to confound the incredulous.

Continuing our perambulation we come presently to Church-Stoke, a pleasant looking village of half-timbered houses seated on the river Camlad, one of them bearing upon its gable-end the inscription, WHAT · IS · HERE · BY · MAN · ERECTED : LET · IT · BE · BY · GOD · PRO-TECTED : IOHN · MIDDLETON · GENT · AN · DO · 1685 : AETATIS · SUÆ · 27 · R · T · C :

Returning direct across the hills to Bishop's Castle, we pass through Broughton, where, it is believed, the Romans had a station. Offa's Dyke, crossing the hills to the westward, runs near to Mainstone, a village supposed to acquire its name from a large granite stone standing near the west gate of the churchyard. From time immemorial it has been the custom for the village youths to test their strength by heaving this stone aloft, and then casting it backwards over the left shoulder. The name of Mainstone, it may be observed, shews the tendency to reduplication in place-names, for Maen is the Welsh for stone. A still more curious instance is that of Dollymase-meadow, near Gloucester, each of the three syllables in this case having exactly the same signification.

The old road from Bishop's Castle to Clun traverses a rough, hilly country, with scarce a place big enough to be called a village all the way. On the outskirts of the town stands Blunden Hall, a timbered mansion, old, but much modernized. Anon our way lies up-hill, with the tree-crowned summit of Bury Ditches rising boldly ahead.

After surmounting a sort of col amidst the dimpled hills, we begin to drop downwards into the vale of Clun, and the little town, with its grey old guardian castle, is seen nestling at the foot of dark, heather-clad hills, where the drifting cloud shadows linger. By-and-bye, as we march past the castle and enter the town, the westward-looking houses are painted in crimson and gold by the glow from the setting sun, while we dusty wayfarers bear away for the Buffalo Inn, whose hospitable roof is to be our shelter to-night.

So taking up our quarters in the Blue Room, we will give the benefit of the doubt to the local legend, and hold that this is the chamber in which Sir Walter Scott once slept, and yonder table the very one upon which the 'Wizard of the North' wrote the first three chapters of 'The Betrothed'—there is nothing like being precise in matters such as these.

Seated upon the banks of the river Clun, on the outskirts of that wild, hilly district to which it gives its name, the quiet market town of Clun forms the chief rendezvous for such slender commerce as goes forward in this isolated part of our County, which time-out-of-mind has acquired the name of Clun Forest.

In early Norman days this remote inaccessible region became a sort of semi-independent Barony, called the 'Honour of Clun,' whose over-lords obtained the royal license to make conquest on the Welsh, and appear to have done pretty much as they liked with the goods and chattels of their unlucky vassals. Nay more, in those 'good old times,' the Lord of Clun claimed the right to inflict capital punishment, for we read of a certain William Kempe holding a messuage and croft on tenure of carrying to Shrewsbury the heads of felons, in order to prove that the right person had been executed.

Save for its ruined Castle and ancient saddle-backed bridge, the townlet is featureless enough; indeed its prim, grey, sober-fronted dwellings look as though they had stepped across from the other side the Welsh border. Yet in bygone times the town must have been a place of no little importance, for we read that, at a survey held in 1605, it was found that 'the town of Clun, through the whole time whereof the memory of man does not exist to the contrary, is an ancient Borough Incorporate, with two Bailiffs, and Burgesses; and the Lord of the town has two Leet Courts, with a View of Frankpledge, held annually by the Seneschal for the time being.'

A bowshot distant from the town rise the ruins of Clun Castle, whose tall, grey, lichen-clad donjon looks out over a horse-shoe bend of the river towards the dark Welsh hills to the westward; even as in the days when Raymond de Berenger, Knight of the Garde Doloreuse, entertained Gwenwyn Prince of Powys in this lonesome fortalice.

Here, at Clun, the FitzAlans lorded it for many a generation over the adjacent march-lands. After many changes and vicissitudes, the castle passed eventually to the present Duke of Norfolk, who from this place acquires his second title of Baron Clun.

With the exception of the keep-tower above mentioned, little remains of Clun Castle save two ruined circular bastions overlooking the river, and certain tall green mounds that give a clue to the original extent of the fortress. The outer bailey with its enclosing vallations is a broad, tree-shaded grassplot, where nowadays the townsfolk go a-pleasuring on high-days and holiday times.

Clun Castle formed a very important link in the chain of fortresses planted by the Normans along the Welsh frontier, to secure their hard-won territory and control the turbulent natives. Towards the close of the twelfth century Rhys, Prince of South Wales, swooped down from his mountain fastnesses, and after many a fierce onslaught stormed and set fire to the castle. At a later period the place fell a prey to that scourge of the Welsh Marches, 'the irregular and wild Glendower,' and was finally dismantled by the Parliamentarians during the Civil Wars. So early, indeed, as the reign of Henry VIII., when that ubiquitous antiquary John Leland journeyed this way, 'Clunne Castell' was 'sumewhat ruinus,' 'though it hath bene,' he adds, 'bothe Stronge and well builded.'

The following lines from 'The Betrothed' have been associated with the Castle of Clun: 'A place strong by nature, and well fortified by art, which the Welch prince had found it impossible to conquer, either by open force or stratagem; and which, remaining with a strong garrison in his rear, often chequed his invasions by rendering his retreat precarious. The river, whose stream washes on three sides the base of the proud eminence on which the castle is situated, curves away from the fortress and its corresponding village on the west, and the hill sinks downward to an extensive plain, so extremely level as to indicate its alluvial origin.

'The bridge, a high narrow combination of arches of unequal size, was about half a mile distant from the castle, in the very centre of the plain. The river itself ran in a deep, rocky channel, was often unfordable, and at all times difficult of passage, giving considerable advantage to the defenders of the Castle.'

Over the old bridge in question lies our way towards Clun church;

Old Lych Gate at Clun.

and, as the local saw has it, 'Whoever crosses Clun Bridge comes back sharper than he went.' The bridge itself, with its five uneven arches and bold sparlings, is still a picturesque object, and in former days was a favourite subject with artists; though the old cordwainer and his ancient timber dwelling beside the bridge have long since passed away.

So we will push ahead to St. George's church, whose massive western tower and curious louvred steeple are already in sight, peering over an old lych-gate in the foreground. This lych-gate is a very charming bit of ancient carpentry, its solid substantial oak beams shewing excellent workmanship, with just a touch of ornamentation here and there; while the roof is covered with rough stone-shingles, overgrown with mosses and lichens.

Passing through the wicket, we traverse a rustic grassgrown God's-acre, beneath the shadow of one of those immemorial yews so common in our country churchyards. Why they were planted in such a situation has afforded no little matter for conjecture; whether they were intended as emblems of immortality, or to serve the more utilitarian purpose of supplying bows for the English archers who in bygone days formed the backbone of our fighting line:

> 'Oh the crooked stick and the grey goose's wing,
> But for which Old England were but a fling!'

The strong nail-studded west door of the church has its old iron hinges, and some names cut in bold Roman letters upon it. The roomy north porch by which we enter has a chamber, or parvise, over it, and stone benches against the walls upon either side. The interior is large and spacious, the fine oak roof being borne upon Norman pillars and arches, while clerestory windows admit light from the southward wall. A modern screen divides nave from chancel, and beside it rises a tall Jacobean pulpit with a sounding-board, all carved in the style peculiar to that period.

The chancel is lighted by well proportioned windows with Purbeck marble shafts. Suspended from the chancel roof hangs a curious fifteenth-century canopy, nicely constructed of oak fashioned into panels, and adorned with three small carved wooden angels. Its purpose is uncertain, but it bears some resemblance to the canopied structure called a baldacchino found in some continental churches.

In the vestry is a mural tablet to Sir Robert Howard; and the rough old staircase leading up into the tower is worth a moment's notice, for the rude simplicity of its construction. The Churchwarden's accounts here shew that, in the year 1741, the sum of ten shillings was paid 'for whipping the Doggs out of ye church, serviss time, and keeping people from sleeping in church During divine serviss.'

In a retired spot upon the eastern side of the town stands the 'Hospital of the Holy and Undivided Trinity at Clunn,' a refuge for decayed tradesmen founded by the Right Hon. the Earl of Northampton, in the year 1614. And truly their lines have fallen in pleasant places, these grey-headed old veterans; each lowly domicile giving upon a central plot of greensward, with benches set against the wall in sunny nooks, and an old wooden pump standing in one corner, with its bucket and chain for drawing water:

> 'The old oaken bucket, the iron-bound bucket,
> The moss-covered bucket which hung in the well.'

'Eh sure, sur,' exclaims an ancient derelict with whom we chance to pass the time of day, 'you'm makin' a purty picture of th'owd plaace, I'll warrand, but I canna see well wi'out my speck-tackles. I binna so young as I was, ye see, but there's several chaps 'ere as is older nor I be, and I'm turned eighty myself.'

A tablet upon the wall of a small chapel, dedicated to the inmates' use, bears a lengthy Latin inscription in memory of Henry Howard, Earl of Northampton, who established similar retreats at Greenwich and Castle Rising.

According to an ordinance duly advertised upon the wall of the dining hall, each poor man is entitled to receive yearly, on Founder's Day, 'a gown ready made of strong cloth or kersey, of a sad colour, to wear upon Week Days; and also every fourth year, upon Trinity Sunday, have delivered unto him to wear, such a livery gown of blue cloth lined

HOSPITAL OF THE
HOLY & UNDIVIDED TRINITY
AT CLUNN.
FOUNDER'S COGNIZANCE.

with bayes, with the Founder's cognizance set on the sleeve, to wear upon Sundays and Festival Days.' In the dining hall, too, is preserved an ancient cross-bow, and a large two-handed double-edged sword about five feet in length.

Such, then, is the old Hospital at Clun; so now, after a moonlight stroll around the environs, we turn in for the night at the 'Buffalo'; and, far removed from the din of railroad shrieks, or bustle of passing traffic, sleep the sleep of the just until morning looks in at the casement.

SEAL OF CLUN HOSPITAL.

ROUND ABOUT CLUN FOREST. TO KNIGHTON AND LUDLOW.

GLANCE at the map at the end of this volume will reveal, down in the south-western extremity of the county, a remote outlying cantle of Shropshire wedged in, as it were, between the Welsh counties of Montgomery and Radnor. It is a wild, hilly, somewhat inaccessible district, even in these days; but in Leland's time the 'faire Forest of Clunne' was 'a great Forest of redde Dere and Roois,' extending over many thousand acres, with much timber growing upon it, and 'very faire and good Game' amongst its holts and hollows.

In and out through this sequestered region wind the clear waters of the Clun, rippling along past rustic crofts and breadths of gorse and fernbrake, and giving its name to a group of quiet villages and hamlets upon its banks:

> 'Clunton and Clunbury, Clungunford and Clun,
> Are the sleepiest places under the sun'—

as the saying goes, though one may vary the epithet ad lib., and substitute drunkenest, dirtiest, etc., as fancy dictates. Towards the south the country falls away to the broader valley of the Teme, which, flowing past Knighton and Coxwall Knoll, forms the southern boundary of the Forest, and parts England from Wales.

Camps, earthworks, etc., dotted plentifully throughout the locality, bear witness to the days when might was the only right, and every man's hand was against his neighbour. Tradition avers that Caractacus made his last stand against the Romans amidst the fastnesses of Clun Forest; and Offa's Dyke, the ancient boundary of Mercia, traverses the district from south to north on its way from Severn to Dee:

> 'There is a faymous thinge
> Calde Offa's Dyke, that reacheth farre in lengthe:
> All kinds of Ware people might thither bringe;
> It was free ground, and calde the Britain's strengthe.'

But it is time to be up and doing, for we must measure many a mile over hill and dale to-day. Old Sol is already abroad, and a light sou' westerly breeze is rustling the fresh young foliage as we fare forth upon our peregrinations; while the thirsty soil emits a grateful smell after the rain of yesternight.

Down the village street, then, we take our way, noticing the legend 'Ironmonger, Dahlia Grower and Poultry Breeder,' over an enterprising tradesman's door. Setting a course up the vale of Clun, we drop into a meadow path that, keeping company with a hollow, waterworn gipsy lane, affords glimpses of the ruined castle, and so brings us presently to Whitcot. Near Whitcot we notice an old grey maenhir, or standing-stone, eight feet high, nearly as broad, and only about six inches in thickness.

With the hills closing in upon either hand we push onwards along the valley, falling into a leisurely pace as the sun warms to his work. Another mile and we come to Offa's Dyke, a huge green mound overshadowed by beech trees, whose course can be easily traced as it crosses the valley and climbs the shaggy hill slope beyond. 'Aye, that's Awf's Ditch, right enough,' says an old fellow tining the hedgerow, 'and now you be in Wales a'this side, like, but it's a cankersome country to live in, I can tell yer.'

At Newcastle we find ourselves in a scattered hamlet overshadowed by certain round green hills, whose topmost crests are scarped with ancient camps or earthworks, whereof the name is legion hereabouts. This part of the Forest, west of Offa's Dyke, was known in olden days as the Manor, or Honour, of Tempseter, a district of Shropshire won from the Welsh before Edward I. was King.

Presently we take leave of the Newtown road, and, crossing the infant Clun at a place called Dyffryn, march away through leafy lanes en route for Bettws-y-Crwyn. Our road goes from bad to worse as it straggles up the bank, degenerating at last into a downright Welsh byway, so that, like Agag of old, we have to 'walk delicately' amidst the ruts and rivulets which do duty as a thoroughfare.

Passing two or three outlying cottages where shock-headed children are playing around the doorways, we come in sight of Bettws-y-Crwyn church, a little lonely fane perched so high aloft on its hill-top as to look down, so to speak, upon every other church throughout the county; indeed with one or two exceptions it is, we believe, the most loftily situated church in England.

The name of this place affords an interesting clue to its history. For Bettws-y-Crwyn, being interpreted, signifies the Bede-house of the Skins; having been so called since, in ancient times, the shepherds who frequented these lonesome hills had a Bede-house or Chapel here, and paid their tribute of skins or hides to Chirbury Priory.

Up here in the churchyard we get a wonderful outlook over the hills and dales of south Shropshire, which are seen stretching away for many a league in picturesque gradation, with Brown Clee Hill bringing up the rear beyond the dark ridges of Wenlock Edge.

We now step inside the church, an ancient timeworn structure whose low grey stone walls, narrow windows and simple bell-cot, look thoroughly in keeping with the circumjacent landscape. The old font, once the pride of the church, was broken into pieces when the church was 'restored' about half a century ago, and used, it is said, to repair the churchyard walls!

By some lucky chance, the ancient rood-screen has escaped the hand of the spoiler, and forms to-day the most notable feature of the little edifice. It is massively constructed of oak grown black with lapse of years, and its gothic arches are wrought into delicate tracery work.

This lofty screen rises to the tie-beam of the roof, whose curved principals, moulded brackets and quatrefoil panels are fashioned, as tradition tells, from Spanish-chestnut wood. Solid oaken benches of

the most primitive construction occupy the nave; their ends displaying the names of various farmhouses, locally termed Halls, such as Hall-of-the-Forest, Moor Hall, Cow Hall, etc.

By favour of the Vicar, we are able to give a sketch of the Bettws Communion cup. It is of silver, bearing the London hall-mark and the date 1662, and is ornamented, as may be seen, with a repoussé flower pattern. Though inferior in design to vessels of an earlier period, such as the beautiful Bacton chalice, this little cup is a very fair example of the silversmith's art of the seventeenth century.

Our way now lies past the vicarage, a modern house standing 'four-square to all the winds of heaven,' and so loftily placed as to be a landmark for miles around. Thence we push on due northwards across the high, open moorlands of Clun Forest, a 'dizzy' country, as they say hereabouts, whose contours are revealed to our sight by shafts of sunlight radiating from the western sky. Patches of golden gorse interspersed amidst bracken and heather fill the air with their warm, rich scent, as we follow the devious trackway; and a shrewd, pungent whiff of peat-reek salutes our nostrils while passing a lonely cottage, for coal is a luxury unknown up here, seven long miles from any railway-station.

CHALICE AT BETTWS Y CRWYN

Old ways and antiquated customs linger yet in this 'back'ardly' neighbourhood, where education has much ado to make headway against ignorance and ancient prejudice. The time-honoured 'Wake' still holds its own in Bettws parish; and rushlights, it is said, are in use to this day in some of the isolated farmhouses towards the Welsh border.

Following a bridle track, we descend into a secluded dell which holds the head waters of the Clun. Then, mounting up through a pine wood, we come out upon the open braeside over against the Cantlin Cross, or Cantlin Stone as it is sometimes called, whose counterfeit presentment appears in our sketch. The cross itself, though handsomely carved, has no particular claims to antiquity, having been erected, as we are informed, about forty years ago by the late Mr. Beriah Botfield, sometime M.P. for Ludlow. The design, however, is evidently an antique one; and on the ground in front of the cross stands a low, flat slab of grey limestone, rudely inscribed with the legend W·C: DECSED · HERE: BVRIED · 1691 · AT · BETVS:

THE CANTLIN CROSS.

The initials are those of a certain William Cantlin, who, travelling through the wilds of Clun Forest in the above mentioned year, met his death at this spot, and was buried at Bettws-y-Crwyn. It is said that upon one occasion the stone itself was produced in a court of law, in order to prove that the place where Cantlin died was situated in the parish of Bettws.

Upon passing through a gate in the adjacent coppice our eyes are gladdened by a vision of folding hills, green fertile vales, and distant cloud - capped mountains, the giants of Wild Wales — a glorious panorama!

Presently we hie away once more upon our travels, retracing our steps to the main road, and swinging along at a good round pace, favoured by the downward grade. Past Hall-of-the-Forest we go, not much of a place, despite its imposing name, though originally built by Anne, Lady Mautravers, some time in the sixteenth century, and hence formerly called Ladye's Hall.

At Newcastle we strike up the hills to the southwards, recrossing old Offa's Dyke and following the crest of the ridge. 'Weather's looking very brewin',' remarks a brother tramp; for storm-clouds, gathering in the west, hover grand and gloomily above the darkening ridges of Radnor Forest; so, putting the best foot foremost, we spin along the grassgrown bridle-path under the lee of the wind-tossed hedgerow. Out leaps the lightning, the thunder rolls, and the tempest swoops down in a whirl of seething rain-scuds; but what care we, for here in the nick of time is the Buffalo Inn at Clun, with a good meat-tea piping hot on the parlour table, and a cheery fire sparkling in the grate.

So while the elements work their will abroad, and the rain drops patter at the casement, we sit within bien and cosy, canopied like gods in clouds of tobacco-smoke; 'fighting our battles o'er again,' and discussing plans of campaign for future excursions amidst 'fresh woods and pastures new.'

* * * * * *

The morrow, then, sees us early astir, and taking the road ere the city man has opened his morning paper. And before the first mile is left behind, we find reason to congratulate ourselves on having made an early start, for the way is parlous steep, and the sun already rejoicing like a giant to run his course. So at a leisurely pace we breast the ascent—'chi va piano va sano,' as the Italians say—with big, rounded hills rising upon either hand, one of them having a strange sort of quarry-like chasm, called the Rock of Woolberry, scored deep in its wooded flank. This collar-work continuing for a matter of two miles or more, brings us to a moorland crest about a thousand feet above sea-level, whence the eye ranges over leagues of broken country, with the play of shine and shadow chequering its varied surface.

At a place bearing the euphemistic title of New Invention, we quit the hard highroad and make a bee-line up the open hillside, until we find ourselves in the vast, prehistoric encampment, known as Gaer Ditches, or Caer Caradoc. The camp proves a fine example of an early British earthwork, being oval, or rather pear-shaped, in form, and protected upon its most vulnerable western flank by three concentric lines of entrenchment; while upon the east, where the natural declivity

is more abrupt, there are but two, with traces of an entrance way in each of these faces.

Tradition has been busy about this interesting spot. We are to believe that once, in days remote, Caractacus stood here at bay against his enemies. Nay, is not the stream at the foot of the hill still called Redlake river, because for three whole days its waters ran red with the blood of the combatants? And down yonder in the vale is

Lurkinghope, where tradition tells the vanquished Britons 'lurked in hope' of retrieving their fortunes, while lying in ambush near the defile at Garn Gap.

However that may have been, we now lay our course for Stow, a tiny hamlet nestling in a wild rocky cirque called Ragged Kingdom. Our route lies over Stow Hill, whose summit is marked by the blackened cairn of the 'Diamond Jubilee' bonfire.

But lusty appetites, begotten of fresh air and hours of steady tramping, now demand instant satisfaction. So down we sit, and, whilst feasting our eyes on the beauties of the landscape, we regale the inner man on more material fare; the pile of sandwiches becoming 'small by degrees, and beautifully less,' as the moments flit by. A drink of clear water under Holloway Rocks, and a pipe or two as we lie on the short, warm turf, and like giants refreshed we go our ways in search of new adventures.

Coming anon to Stow, we borrow the key from the neighbouring vicarage, and armed with this 'open sesame' proceed forthwith to the church.

This diminutive house of prayer has one or two notable features. A good open-timbered roof spans the nave, traces of a rood-loft being visible overhead where it joins the chancel, though no approach to it can now be discovered. A massive oak communion table is about the only remnant of ancient fittings here. A small wooden bell-cot rises above the western gable, and the walls of the church, which are unusually thick, are pierced with modernized windows.

Bidding adieu to this lofty yet lowly hamlet, we traverse a narrow green lane where the hedgerows are a-tangle with dog-roses, briony and 'traveller's-joy,' besides many another familiar wayside wildling. In two miles we find ourselves at Knighton, a pleasant, busy townlet, just within the Radnorshire border.

Here we board the first up-train that comes along; the railway line hugging the frontier, and affording glimpses of the hill country amidst which we have recently wandered. Near Bucknall station we catch sight of Coxwall Knoll, an isolated tree-clad monticle surrounded by ancient entrenchments, where some authorities locate the scene of Caractacus's last tussle with Ostorius. Bucknall village is close at hand on the brink of the Redlake river, its grey church tower just peeping over the trees that clothe the hills in the background. There is a curious old font in Bucknall church with a sort of interlacing pattern carved around its bowl, the date whereof is uncertain.

Running past Bedstone, we alight at Hopton Heath station, shoulder sketching gear, etc., and trudge away to Heath House, which lies a short mile to the southward. Heath House, the residence of Chas. Seaton, Esq., is a large, substantial edifice, dating mainly from the latter part of the seventeenth century, and seated in a broad park-like demesne.

The interior of the mansion contains several handsome, panelled apartments, adorned with pictures and curios that reflect the artistic taste of their present proprietor. But the most notable feature of the house is an elaborate old staircase hung with ancient tapestry, which, as may be gathered from our sketch, is a marvel of massive construction. Its huge oaken handrails and newels, and even the twisted balusters, look as strong and simple as possible, and much of the work has the appearance of having been fashioned with the axe. The topmost flight of all, said to have been brought from Hopton Castle, is little better than a ladder in point of convenience.

Broadward Hall, the next-door neighbour to Heath House, is a plain stone building chiefly remarkable from the fact that it is built, so to say, around a curious circular staircase. In the grounds abutting upon the river Clun rises an artificial tump, surmounted by a group of lofty elm trees. Via Broadward Bridge we now make our way to Clungunford; diverging a little to take a look at Beckjay Mill, in bygone days a favourite haunt of David Cox, the artist.

Clungunford village, rambling beside the river Clun, has a well-restored church, flanked by a prehistoric tumulus. St. Cuthbert's church is well worth a visit, for its ancient features have been faithfully preserved, including one of those singular 'leper' windows that have so often proved a bone of contention to archæologists.

On a sunny bank overlooking the river Clun stands Clungunford House, the residence of J. C. L. Rocke, Esq., Lord of the Manor.

STAIRCASE AT HEATH HOUSE, CLUNGUNFORD. H.T.T.

Half a mile away upstream is Abcott Manor-house, a large old half-timbered structure now used as a farmhouse. A big, curiously moulded chimney stack, is a noticeable object as we draw near; and, being shewn within, we pass from one old dilapidated chamber to another, admiring its wainscoted walls and plastered ceilings, which, beautiful even in decay, still display queer heraldic monsters, lions, stags, unicorns, goats, parrots, etc., engaged amidst interlacing strap-work. One or two old lattice-paned windows here retain their original wrought-iron fastenings.

Abcott was for many generations the abode of the Princes, a family now extinct in this locality, though there are monuments in plenty to them in Clungunford church.

The Rocke Arms at the end of the village is a rustic inn of the homely, oldfashioned sort, quite equal to providing a pint and a chop, or finding, at a pinch, a night's lodging for the passing traveller. So here we call a halt awhile to refresh the inner man, before tackling the cross-country lanes that are to lead us to Hopton Castle. Pleasant it is, as one jogs along these rural byways, to see the country children curtseying to the stranger as he passes, a custom all too rapidly falling into desuetude in these 'independent' days, when young brains are crammed with undigested facts, while the character is left to make shift as best it may.

In a nook of the hills to the westward stands Hopton Castle, a grey old Norman keep-tower, seated in a curiously low exposed position near the banks of a stream. Traces of ruined outworks indicate that the place was much more extensive in former days, when it figured in some stirring episodes of March-land history. By Camden's account, Hopton was presented by Henry II., to Walter de Clifford, of Clifford Castle in Herefordshire; and towards the end of the thirteenth century we find Roger, Lord Mortimer, of Wigmore, in possession of the Castle. Passing later to the Corbets and the Wallops, Hopton Castle held out stubbornly for the King at the time of the Civil Wars, but in 1644 was captured and demolished by the Parliamentarians, its garrison put to the sword, and Samuel Moor the Governor marched off to prison at Ludlow Castle.

A curious old grant, by right of which the 'Heyres-mayle of ye Hoptons' held this Manor of William the Conqueror, runs to the following effect:

> 'I, Will, King, the third of my reign,
> Give to the Northern Hunter,
> To me that art both Luine and Deare,
> The Hoppe, and the Hoptoune,
> And all the bounds, up and downe,
> Under the Earth to Hell,
> Above the Earth to Heaven,' etc.

Returning by a different route direct to Hopton Heath station, we pass through Broome, 'change' upon arriving at Craven Arms, and run down past Stokesay Castle to Onibury, whose church has an ancient, possibly pre-Norman, chancel arch, and one or two other good features. On the outskirts of the village stands Stokesay Court, the handsome modern residence of H. J. Allcroft, Esq., Lord of the Manor, and owner of large estates in this locality.

Alighting at Bromfield station we make our way to the village, as picturesque a spot as one could wish to see, situated in a pleasant, fertile vale, close to the place where Onny and Teme unite. At the end of the village street we traverse an old, grey, many-arched bridge, spanning the lively Onny, near which rises a row of lofty, storm-rent poplars, still known as the 'Twelve Apostles,' though several veterans have succumbed to the gales in recent years.

A furlong further on we espy a picturesque old building pierced by a wide stone archway, and chequered with timber quarterings, over which a fine elm tree casts its dappled shadow. This was the Gatehouse of Bromfield Priory, a Benedictine monastery, whose history carries us very far back into the 'queer old crumpled-up past,' for the annals of Domesday Book shew that, even in the Conqueror's time, Bromfield was a place of some consequence.

Originally a college of secular canons, the monastery became later on an establishment of Canons regular of the Benedictine order; receiving benefits at the hands of King Henry II., in whose reign Bromfield Priory became affiliated to St. Peter's Abbey at Llanthony Secunda, near Gloucester.

Bromfield church, whether regarded as a prominent feature in a fair landscape, or examined in the details of its architecture, cannot but afford the visitor much pleasant matter for contemplation. Seated upon one of those waterside meads the monks of old so frequently selected, its broad, massive tower and weather-stained gables are seen mirrored in the stream that winds around the churchyard, and with the ancient Priory ruins, flanked by a group of dark firs rising clear against the sky, makes a charming study for the artists' brush.

Internally, too, the church has many points of interest. The chancel arch of the old Priory church may be discerned in the eastern wall, the chancel itself having been pulled down when the parish came into possession. A remarkably handsome modern triptych is a noticeable feature of the church, contrasting favourably with the plaster ceiling overhead, whose colour-decorations have been aptly described as 'the best specimen of the worst period of ecclesiastical art.'

Crossing the Teme by an old stone bridge, we enter Oakley Park, a glorious stretch of ferny glades and secluded woodland dingles, boasting such Druid oaks as it would be hard to match elsewhere. Right ahead rise the richly timbered slopes of Bringwood Chase, a picturesque range of hills, whose topmost crests are crowned by three conspicuous clumps of trees, landmarks for miles around. Oakley Hall, a red-brick Georgian mansion, lies off upon our left, and is chiefly remarkable for its uncommonly beautiful situation on the banks of the Teme, overlooking some of the choicest scenery in the district.

Away towards Downton lie certain parcels of land known to this day as 'Crawl Meadows,' and thereby hangs the following tale. Once upon a time, a certain fair maid having plighted her troth with a valiant but impecunious knight, the angry sire vowed her sole dower should be just so much land as his daughter could crawl over, on hands and knees, between sun-set and dawn of day. Commencing her journey at Bromfield, the young lady travelled with such vigour that, by the time old Sol peeped over the hills again, she was well on her way to Downton, a good four miles, as the crow flies, from her starting-place at Brômfield.

But the waning daylight warns us to be astir, while the towers of Ludlow Castle, rising darkly against the eastward sky, tell we are within a measurable distance of our journey's end.

So betwixt fields and hedgerows we now hasten along, exchanging a 'good e'en' with the cottagers as we trudge through a wayside hamlet, and coming to a bridge over Teme, where the last of the daylight flickers upon the waters of a rushing weir. Then up a steep way through Dinham, passing a dusky old building, now a coach-house, but once a Gothic chapel, and rounding the outskirts of the castle; the homing rooks in the elms overhead announcing our arrival in their own vociferous fashion.

Thus through narrow, crowded, old-fashioned streets, we come to our night's bivouac at Ludlow; promising ourselves a treat on the morrow in exploring the memory-haunted precincts of this historic border-town.

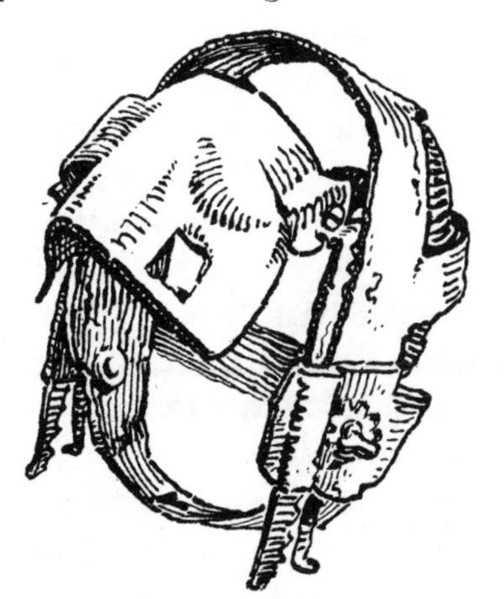

BRANKS AT LUDLOW.

ROUND ABOUT LUDLOW.

UDLOW town occupies a fine, commanding situation upon a sort of knoll, or promontory of high land, encompassed upon its southern side by the windings of the Teme, whose waters, flowing through a picturesque defile beneath the limestone scarps of Whitcliff, here divide Shropshire from its neighbour of Hereford.

What the place was like in olden times we may gather from the records of John Leland. 'The town of Ludlow,' he observes, writing in the reign of Henry VIII., 'is very propre, welle walled and gated, and standeth every way eminent from a Botom. In the side of the Town, as a Peace of the Enclosing of the Walle, is a fair Castel. Within the Town, even yn the mydle, is one Paroch chyrch. There be in the Wall 5 gates. Broad gate leadeth to Broad Street, the fayrest part of the Towne. The Castel standeth on a strong Rocke, well ditched, between Corne gate and Mille gate. The Paroch church is very fayre and large, and richly adorned, and taken for the fayrest in all those Quarters.'

The town, then, as Leland has it, 'standeth every way eminent from a Botom,' with the noble old church of St. Lawrence crowning the brow of the hill, so that its tall, ruddy tower forms a notable landmark to the good folks of the whole countryside.

Upon the western flank of the town, just where the declivity is most precipitous, rise the ruins of Ludlow Castle; that magnificent stronghold of the Lords Marchers, to which the place owes its ancient fame. To the Castle, then, let us first of all direct our steps.

Sir Henry Sydney's Gateway, Ludlow Castle.

Approaching by way of Castle Square, we enter upon a broad, smooth stretch of greensward, encompassed by stone walls and old ruined structures, the Base court or outer Bailey of the fortress. Before us rises a noble pile of buildings which constitute the main fabric of the castle. Grey and weatherworn, shrouded in ivy, and overshadowed by tall sycamore trees, these venerable ruins compose a scene picturesque to a degree, whereof the sketch upon the opposite page may convey some impression.

Ludlow Castle & Church.

In the centre rises the great Keep or donjon tower, a vast substantial structure of the Norman period, whose massive walls, pierced with narrow, round-arched openings, little better than loopholes, contrast strikingly with the mullioned windows and slender, roofless gables that appear alongside. These latter, as is recorded by an inscription above the entrance gateway, owe their inception to Sir Henry Sydney, President of the Welsh Marches in the reign of Queen Elizabeth, whose arms, conjoined with those of England and France, appear in a panel above the archway, with the date of erection, 1581.

An isolated tower away to the left is one of the most ancient portions of the castle. It is known as 'Mortimer's Tower,' from a tradition that Hugh de Mortimer was imprisoned within its walls towards the close of the twelfth century. But that is another story, whereof more anon.

Let us now pass on to the inner ward, which is surrounded by tall, irregular structures, whose crumbling walls and battlements have been brought to a rare state of soft, harmonious colouring, by the mellowing touch of time.

Out in the courtyard, detached from all its neighbours, rises a small circular twelfth-century chapel, whose beautifully enriched, semi-headed west doorway and curiously carved string-course, bespeak the Normans' handiwork. This chapel is almost unique of its kind in England. The fine chancel arch still remains, but of the chancel itself only the foundations can now be traced. In former days the chapel was hung with 'Armes in colours, sitch as fewe can shewe,'

> 'So bravely wroughte, so fayre and finely fram'd,
> That to the Worlde's end their beauty may endure !'

We now pass out again into the green courtyard. Turning our backs upon the entrance way we see before us an extensive group of buildings, now roofless and half in ruin, yet stately in their decay. In the centre, approached by a sort of sloping gangway, rises a noble hall, a spot famed in local history as the scene of the earliest performance of Milton's 'Masque of Comus.' One of the adjacent chambers is pointed out as that occupied by Prince Arthur, son of Henry VII.

Beside the Keep-tower are the scanty ruins of the castle kitchen, which, to judge from the fireplace, an enormous oven, and some rusty iron utensils of proportionate size, must have been on a scale commensurate even with the needs of this vast mediæval ménage. Close at hand is the castle well, which, though not enclosed within the area of the Norman keep, is not far away from it, and was probably protected by its adjacent outworks.

Down in the basement of the keep is a dark, vaulted chamber, far below the surface of the ground. This was originally used as the castle chapel, whereof two well-proportioned Norman arches still remain, supported upon slender pillars with simply ornamented capitals. A curious arrangement of walls and passages here has given rise to an obscure myth concerning lions, or other wild beasts, having been kept in this chamber to devour obnoxious prisoners, when it was used at one time as a dungeon.

Well, to make a long story short, a climb to the top of the ancient Keep-tower forms a fitting finale to our explorations; for the prospect from its lofty battlements is extremely varied and picturesque. The castle precincts, lying at our feet, look very green and pleasant amid their setting of verdant foliage. Beyond a group of tall elms appear the old tiled roofs of the town, dominated by the stately tower of St. Lawrence's church, while the bold outline of Titterstone Clee Hill rises far away in the background. Towards the north lie the Stretton hills, enclosing a luxuriant vale, followed by the dimpled heights that mark the whereabouts of Clun Forest. Directing our gaze towards the south, a goodly scene meets the eye where the Teme, winding through its hollow gorge, washes the lower slopes of Whitcliff, whose rough, rocky terraces merge higher up in the rich masses of woodland that clothe the hillsides.

Many a time in the dim, forgotten past, have these old walls re-echoed to the making of history. At the date of Domesday Survey the Manor of Ludlow was held by Roger de Lacy, by whom the Castle was built.

Joce de Dinan, 'a strong and valiant knight,' who was Lord of Ludlow in King Stephen's reign, was constantly at feud with his rival, Hugh de Mortimer of Wigmore, until, having captured that knight by an ambuscade, he shut him up a prisoner in the loftiest tower in the third ward of the Castle, which to this day retains the name of 'Mortimer's Tower.'

Under King Stephen and his successor the fortress passed through a time of storm and stress, marked by some stirring incidents. A romantic story turns upon the adventures of Fulk FitzWarine and

Hawyse, daughter of Joce de Dinan; and the intrigues of Arnold de Lisle with that 'very gentle damsel,' Marion of the Heath.

Early in the thirteenth century Ludlow Castle was seized by King John, who, during his great struggle with the Barons, carried fire and sword throughout the Welsh Marches. Henry III. visited Ludlow in the course of his Border wars, and concluded there a treaty of peace with Prince Llewelyn. During this and the succeeding reign the Mortimers, Lords of Wigmore, attained to great influence, and eventually secured by marriage their claim to the English crown.

Richard Plantagenet, during his chequered career, was often at Ludlow Castle, where he was besieged by the King in October, 1459. Treachery in the camp, however, proved the ruin of Richard's cause, and the Lancastrians captured and plundered the castle.

After suffering eclipse, the fortunes of York were once more retrieved at the famous Battle of Mortimer's Cross, fought a few miles from Ludlow. At a later date Edward IV. sent his two boys for safe keeping to Ludlow Castle; and Arthur Tudor, Prince of Wales, son of Henry VII., spent a portion of his short life within its precincts.

The Court of the Presidency of Wales, established about this period, figures largely in the subsequent history of Ludlow; and by the middle of the sixteenth century the town and castle had risen to the zenith of their fortunes. At the time of the Civil Wars Ludlow Castle was held for the King, and proved a hard nut for the Parliamentarians to crack, being the last stronghold in Shropshire to fall into their hands. In 1689 the Court of the Marches was abolished, and as a result the Castle was finally allowed to fall into a state of ruin and decay.

A truce, now, to history. Retracing our steps to the castle-garth, we pass through the outer doorway and fare forth into Ludlow town in search of antiquarian spoil. Our quest is quickly rewarded, for at yonder street corner, beyond some tall elms, rises the Castle Lodge, a picturesque structure of timber and plaster, built by Thomas Sackford, a burgess of Ludlow, in Queen Elizabeth's reign. Sackford held the office of Master of Requests under that Sovereign, and in 1572 was appointed Porter, and Keeper of the Prisoners in the Marches of Wales. The ancient timber quartering of the upper story has only recently been brought to light from beneath its coating of modern plaster; a laudable restoration, which might well be imitated in the case of other old Ludlow house-fronts.

In Castle Square, hard by, stands the new Market-house, a spick-and-span production of the 1887 Jubilee year. Its older prototype was a plain, unobtrusive brick edifice dating from the time of Queen Anne; of which period one or two large, roomy houses, overlooking Castle Square, are fair representatives.

Threading our way through a narrow thoroughfare, we presently catch a glimpse of a quaint old structure, surmounted by a clock turret, or belfry. This is the Butter Cross, a grey stone edifice built, perhaps, a couple of centuries ago, and, without any great pretensions to architectural taste, yet a pleasant object to look upon by reason of its uneven, weather-stained surfaces, and rough irregular contours. Beneath its old worn arches the country folk foregather of a market day; and it is worth while to linger near on a Sunday morning to watch the Mayor's procession, when, accompanied by the black robed mace-bearers, he marches hence to attend service in the great collegiate church hard by, as the time-honoured custom is. Let us follow his Worship's lead, then, and take a look at St. Lawrence's church.

For this purpose we turn through a short narrow passage-way, which goes by the curious name of 'Scallens,' or Kalends; at the end whereof we find ourselves before a large hexagonal south porch with angle buttresses and embattled parapet, a feature seldom met with in our English churches.

St. Lawrence's church at Ludlow is undoubtedly one of the finest throughout all broad Shropshire. Its ruddy sandstone walls, its serried buttresses and graceful flamboyant windows, rise in charming contrast above the sombre yew trees whose foliage enshrouds the quiet graveyard; while, high overhead, the great central tower soars aloft into the blue, with the jackdaws wheeling and circling around its topmost battlements, or holding noisy conclave amidst the intricacies of its great traceried windows.

The interior of the church, too, displays that spacious dignity characteristic of the Perpendicular style; the clerestoried nave, the chancel with its grand painted windows, and the lofty open lantern beneath the tower, combining to create an appearance of cathedral-like magnificence. What with the rich, subdued glow of ancient glass, the dark oak screens spanning chancel and transepts, and the slender pillars and arches soaring far aloft, the general effect is extremely noble and impressive.

A magnificent canopied oak rood-screen divides the nave from the chancel, which is flanked on either side by rows of stalls, used in bygone times by the chantry priests of St. John of Jerusalem, their dark oaken tracery contrasting beautifully with the old grey stonework around. The miserere seats here are worth a close examination, being carved with very quaint emblematical imagery; as, for example, the panel which figures at the end of the present chapter.

The great Perpendicular window, which occupies nearly the whole of the east end of the chancel, is filled with ancient stained glass, portraying, in the realistic style dear to the mediæval mind, scenes from the Legend of St. Lawrence, the tutelary saint of the church.

Some good old glass in the east window of the adjacent chapel of St. John records the so-called Legend of the Ring. The treatment is curious and original, as it often was in those days. Indeed, every window of this chapel has some beauty of its own.

But to return to the chancel. Beneath the great window, from wall to wall, extends an elegant stone reredos, brought to light some years since in the course of restorations. It is divided up into a series of canopied and crocketed niches, containing small sculptured statues of considerable beauty. Behind this screen is a remarkable little chamber lighted by a single early pointed window, and supposed to have been used either as the church-treasury, or for communicating with lepers, or outcasts.

In the south chancel wall there is a handsome sedilia of Perpendicular date; and opposite to it a large, arched recess, where the Easter Sepulchre was displayed in pre-Reformation days.

The south or Lady-chapel has a fine Jesse window, besides other notable features. The backs of the stalls, dividing this chapel from the chancel, are painted in Old English lettering with 'The commandemente of Almyghty God,' set up, by order of the royal commissioners, in the reign of good Queen Bess. In olden times it was customary for the Cordwainers and other honourable companies to hold their meetings in this chapel; as did the Fletchers, or Arrowsmiths, in the north transept, the gable whereof is still surmounted by their cognizance, an arrow. An unusually fine flamboyant window is, unfortunately, hidden from the interior by the large and very excellent organ that almost monopolizes this transept.

Though not so numerous as one might expect, there are several handsome monuments in Ludlow church. The oldest of these is a much mutilated table-tomb in the north aisle, reputed to be that of Arthur, Prince of Wales, son of Henry VII., who died near Ludlow. On the top of this tomb are piled, and doled out thence every Sunday morning, twelve goodly quartern loaves for the benefit of as many poor widows.

Under the before-mentioned arch of the Easter Sepulchre, upon a panelled table-tomb, repose the effigies of an Elizabethan knight and his lady, with the ensuing inscription: 'HEARE LYETH THE BODYES OF SYR ROBART TOWNESHEND, KNIGHT, CHIEF JUSTES OF THE COUNSELL IN THE MARCHES OF WALLES AND CHESTER, AND DAME ALICE HYS WYFF.' In the panels below appear their 'VI. SONNES AND VI. DOUGHTERS, LAWFULLY BEGOT.'

Over the way is a similar but plainer tomb, which, though now lacking the 'Closet fayre in-wrought, where Lords may sit in stately solemn wise,' that Churchyard the poet saw, displays still some handsome hatchments, set into the wall above. 'HEARE LYETHE,' runs the legend, 'THE BODYE OF AMBROSIA SYDNEY, IIIITH DOUGHTER OF THE RIGHT HONORABLE SYR HENRYE SYDNEY, KNIGHT OF THE MOSTE

NOBLE ORDER OF THE GARTER, LORDE PRESIDENT OF THE COUNSELL OF WALLES, ETC., AND OF THE LADYE MARYE, HYS WYEF, DOUGHT[E] OF Y[E] FFAMOUS DUKE OF NORTHUMBERLAND, WHO DYED IN LUDLOWE CASTELL, Y[E] 22ND OF FEBRUARI, 1574.'

An adjacent monument to Edmund Walter and his lady, dated 1592, shews traces of a degenerate style creeping in, Time with his hour-glass appearing atop of the arch, with scrolls and pediments introduced by way of enrichments.

This sort of funereal gear, so much in vogue at a later period, is well seen upon the eighteenth-century memorial to Theophilus Salwey, Esq., with its chubby, smiling cherub, placidly seated upon an hour-glass, and surrounded by skulls, bones, and suchlike disjecta membra, a curious conjunction! Salwey, with equal mind, declares himself by the inscription, 'Pro Rege Sæpe, Pro Republica Semper.'

The antiquary may discover much matter of this sort in the course of a stroll through St. Lawrence's church; but, not to pursue the subject ad nauseam, we will now sally forth into the town again, and continue our peregrinations. Before leaving the church, however, let us glance at the ancient font, a strange, archaic-looking stone vessel, large, plain and bowl-shaped, and bearing traces of the days when it did duty as a watering trough somewhere in the vicinity.

Once more in the open air we turn towards the east end of the churchyard, where the ancient abode known as the Reader's House raises its old weatherbeaten gable beside the pathway; a delightful jumble of rough stonework, carved beams and dim, diamond-paned windows. The low portal, enclosing an ancient nail-studded door, is beautiful with rare old Jacobean carving, and a row of plain brick dwellings alongside contrast not unpleasingly with their venerable neighbour.

A terraced walk on the north side of the churchyard occupies the site of the old town wall, and embraces a fair prospect over the surrounding country, a goodly, fertile landscape, very pleasant to behold. In ancient times, before the Normans built their church on the site of the present edifice, a prehistoric tumulus occupied the western end of what is now the graveyard. From this monticle the town is said to acquire its name, the word Ludlow being derived from Leod-hlaw, the People's Hill, shewing the place is at least as old as Saxon times.

Of the 'fayre House' of the Palmers' Guild 'at the west end of the Paroche Churche-yard,' there are some scanty remains incorporated amidst more modern buildings, now not easy to find, nor yet very imposing when discovered. And as for the 'Hospitall or Almes-house of a 30 poore Folke,' built by one Hosyer in the year of grace 1468, and noticed by Leland, its place is now usurped by the gaunt red-brick edifice opposite the west front of the church.

PALMERS GUILD, LUDLOW.

We now retrace our steps to the Butter Cross, calling to mind old Churchyard's lines on Ludlow:

> 'Who that lists to walk the Towne about
> Shall find therein some rare and pleasant things.'

Yonder before us lies Broad Street, a spacious, respectable-looking thoroughfare still, if not as in Leland's time, 'the fayrest part of the Towne;' with Butcher Row under the pillars to the left, the Angel Hotel farther on, and the solitary survivor of Ludlow's seven town-gates spanning the lower end of the street.

So down Broad Street we now take our way, pausing beneath the grim old archway to notice the grooves for the portcullis in its massive masonry. Two semicircular towers, jutting boldly forth, protect the gateway upon its outer side, and command the approach from Ludford Bridge. Sober, antiquated tenements cling like parasites around the ancient gateway, and the humble Wheat-Sheaf Inn thrusts out its bar-parlour window upon the site of the old town moat.

A bowshot farther we come to Ludford Bridge; and, as in Leland's day, 'there be three fayre arches in this bridge over Teme,' though the 'pretty chapel upon it of St. Catherine' is now no more. Huge sparlings, wider than the bridge itself, afford tempting nooks wherein to linger and gaze upon the clear tide swirling past the bold cutwaters below, where house-leeks, ground-ivy and such-like wildlings, have made their homes in the crannies of the stonework.

The view hence is delightful, look which way we will; trees, rocks, bustling rapids and deep, calm pools that reflect the sky, combining to form a scene of rural harmony. A picturesque old flour-mill and some dilapidated tanneries still cling to the bank hard by, though Peter Undergod's ancient fulling-mill is now a thing of the past, having been swept away in an unprecedented flood a dozen years ago.

Beyond the bridge rise the church, the ancient manor-house and timbered cottages of Ludford, a fascinating spot; but Ludford lies without our province, in shire Hereford. So turning presently to the right-about, we leave upon our dexter hand the site of an Hospital, founded by Peter Undergod in King John's reign and dedicated to St. John Baptist, whereof the name alone now survives. Then, passing through Broad Gate again, we strike thence into a narrow lane running alongside the old town-wall.

This brings us to Mill Street, near a row of humble stone tenements wherein Mr. Oliver Baker discovered, some few years ago, traces of old work dating back as far as the thirteenth century. These are supposed to be the remains of Barnaby House, a guest-house where, in mediæval times, pilgrims used to break their journey when travelling into Wales.

Arrived in Mill Street, we make for the Grammar School, a long, low, whitewashed building relieved by dormer windows, and retaining, in a couple of two-light trefoil-headed windows and a wide arched doorway, relics of antiquity. It is a place of very early foundation, having been established by the Palmers' Guild in the thirteenth century, and afterwards made over to the Ludlow Corporation with the stipulation that they 'alwayes finde in ye same Towne, at their own charges, a free Grammar schole, with a schoolmaster and an Hussher, for the erudicion of youth in the Latine tonge.' Chartered by King Edward VI., the School, one of the most ancient in the Kingdom, still continues its useful and prosperous career.

The Ludlow Natural History Society has a small but well arranged

THE "FEATHERS" HOTEL, LUDLOW.

Museum near the top of Mill Street, which is replete with objects of interest to the antiquary and the naturalist.

Here, in the district where they were originally brought to light, the famous fossils of Siluria may be studied; while birds, fishes, and shells of various kinds are well in evidence. Then there are the relics of bygone Ludlow, a curious olla podrida; here a rusty iron-bound deed-chest, there a quaint money-box with intricate lock; or something 'loathely and grim' in the way of torturing gear, such as the Branks shewn in the sketch at the end of the foregoing chapter, a horrid engine used for compressing the heads and branding the cheeks of malefactors.

Upon the wall above the Museum door hang two big wooden balls, with a rope's-end attached to each. These were used in olden times upon Shrove Tuesday, when a kind of municipal tug-of-war took place. At either end of a long rope (whereof we here see the remnants) the men of Broad and Castle Wards confronted the champions of Corve Street and Old Street, each party endeavouring to pull their opponents over to their side of the town, until the end of the rope went into the Teme or the Corve, as the tide of contest swayed.

The Butter Cross is once again our rendezvous. Passing thence towards the Bull Ring, we notice several fine old timber-framed houses, besides others that hide their charms beneath a disfiguring mantle of whitewash. Some of these ancient residences retain their handsome plaster ceilings, and oaken staircases with massive newels and twisted balusters.

The Bull Ring itself, where our 'rude forefathers' enjoyed the exhilarating sport of bull-baiting, is encumbered with some oldish houses, not bad ones of their kind. But such attractions as they offer are quite put into the shade by a beautiful half-timbered edifice which rises but a stone's-throw away, so thitherward let us now direct our steps.

This is the Feathers Hotel, an ancient hostelry which, as may be gathered from our sketch, is a magnificent example of mediæval domestic architecture. Observe how the venerable house seems to 'stand at ease,' as it were, in these days of its ripe old age; its tall beetling gables and quaintly carved beams leaning this way or that, quite regardless of perspective. With what picturesque effect its diamond-paned oriel windows jut forth from beneath the deep-browed eaves, and the queer carven monsters ogle the passer-by from bulging bracket and beam end; and how charmingly the flowering creepers on the balcony relieve its grim old timbers.

Upon stepping within we notice the letters R.I. on the lock-plate of the door; but whether this refers to King James I., or to Mr. Jones, the traditional builder of the house, we leave others to decide. The same letters reversed figure upon the beautiful carved oak chimney-piece in the coffee-room, which, with its elaborate plaster ceiling, intricately carved oak panelling, and low, lattice-paned windows, has quite a mediæval appearance. Hard by is another fine wainscoted chamber, where some visitor of bygone days has set his signet in the form of a family hatchment, duly 'erased' and 'impaled,' in true heraldic fashion.

In point of historic interest, the record of this fine old hostelry is little better than a 'perfect and absolute blank.' But from the general style of its architecture, and the presence of the royal arms in its principal chamber, it has been conjectured that The Feathers was in some way connected with the Courts of the Marches, which played such an important part at Ludlow in mediæval days.

Over the way stands The Bull, another oldfashioned hotel, with one of those large, rambling inn-yards, familiar to travellers of a bygone generation. Upstairs in the dining-room are preserved those 'armes in colours, sitch as fewe can shewe,' which, as we have seen, once graced the ancient castle chapel; and amongst them may be found the armorial bearings of many a one who bore a name to conjure with in the brave days of old.

Thomas Lane, in the year 1674, established at Ludlow an almshouse for aged and decayed women. Its habitat in Old Street is still known as Lane's Asylum, a picturesque structure of timber and stone displaying the half obliterated letters E.C. upon a gable-end, and a date that looks like 1621. The house itself is evidently of great age, but has nothing of interest within, save and except an old coat-of-arms in the refectory, supported by the lion and winged griffin, and ensigned by a royal crown and the initials E.R.

Of the Whitefriars Monastery, that 'fayre and costly thinge' which Leland noticed on the banks of Corve, scarce one stone has been left upon another; or, to speak more precisely, one solitary arch stands tottering to its fall. Being far gone into disrepair, the place was pulled down about a century ago, and its materials carted away to build pigstys and the like.

In the same quarter is to be seen a group of ancient almshouses built by one of the Foxes of Bromfield, whose coat-of-arms, with the date 1593, appears upon the low grey stone façade fronting on the highway.

Thus it will be seen that, hidden away amongst the nooks and corners of Ludlow town, there are many relics of ancient domestic architecture, such as lend a quaint, mediæval appearance to its older streets. The surrounding country, too, is equally favoured, for it is full of the charm of secluded, rural beauty; while rustic villages and smiling homesteads are to be met with on every hand.

So now let us bid farewell to the pavements, and, taking to the leafy lanes, push forth again into the open country.

A 'Misserere' at Ludlow.

THE CLEE HILLS, CORVE DALE, AND WENLOCK EDGE.

AWAY to the north-east, as we turn our backs upon Ludlow, appears a noble range of hills, whereof we have caught frequent glimpses during our peregrinations about the old town. And now, as we fare along through a pleasant, pastoral country, the dark, volcanic-looking crest of Titterstone Clee Hill looms grandly above the rolling woodlands that clothe his lower flanks.

'Cle Hills,' as Leland informs us, 'be holy in Shropshire. The highest Parte of Cle Hills is cawlyd Tyderstone. In it is a fayre playne grene, and a fountaine in it. There is another Hill a 3 Miles distant from it cawlyd the Brown Cle.'

Geologically these hills are somewhat remarkable. A cap of erupted basalt crowns the summits of the Clees, having by its harder texture protected the hills from the effects of denudation, and preserved from destruction the underlying coal measures that now form the loftiest coal-field in Britain. Hence it comes to pass that, in these utilitarian days, the 'fayre playne grene and the fountaine' have given place to coalpits, and to those yawning stone quarries that yield the famous road metal locally known as 'Dhu stone.'

Leaving the old timbered farmhouse of Dodmore upon our left, we descend into a pleasant vale, cross the Ledwych brook and bear away for Bitterley; following a narrow, unfrequented lane, with Titterstone making a brave show in the direction whither we are bound.

Set amidst green summer foliage, Bitterley village looks attractive enough as we traverse its one quiet thoroughfare; but in winter-time, as the name suggests, the district is bleak and chilly:

> 'Bitterley, Bitterley under the Clee,
> Devil take me if I ever come to thee!'

runs a rustic couplet that tells its own tale.

At the farther end of the village we turn aside to examine an old, ruinous pile, rising forlorn and derelict in the midst of an adjacent

THE HAUNTED HOUSE, BITTERLEY.

meadow. Upon nearer acquaintance this proves to be an ancient, dilapidated edifice, in the last stages of decay. With its time-stained brick walls and crow-stepped gables smothered in untended ivy, the mullioned windows agape to every gale, and roof and chimneys tottering to their fall, the old place looks a haunted house, every inch of it, as our sketch will shew.

A solid oak newel staircase 'corkscrews' upwards in a projecting turret, but, save a few remnants of elaborate stucco ornamentation above the fireplace in one desolate chamber, there is little or nothing to repay

CROSS AT BITTERLEY.

the risk of a broken neck. So, remarking certain traces of a moat in the meadow hard by (restored by 'artist's license' in the sketch), we now hie away through lanes and fields to Bitterley church.

Bitterley church and the old Court-house, with some noble trees in the foreground and Titterstone towering behind, make a pleasing rural picture as we draw near; and, upon passing through the wicket and entering the green sanctuary, we come in sight of the beautiful churchyard Cross shewn in the adjoining sketch. It dates from the Decorated period, the slender shaft rising from a flight of worn, mossy steps, and bearing aloft the four-sided head, or finial, in whose crocketed niches some mouldering fragments of sculptured work may still be discerned. This Cross is one of the finest of its kind in England.

The church itself is of Norman origin, though much altered in later times. The best features of the interior are a fine arcaded Norman font, a curious old lectern and iron-bound muniment chest, and slight remains of a traceried oak roodscreen.

Beyond Bitterley church the country opens out towards the unenclosed flanks of Titterstone Clee Hill :

> 'Those mountains of commande
> The Clees, like loving twins, and Stitterstone that stande
> Transevered,'

—as the poet Drayton hath it. So, putting the best foot foremost, we have a lung-expanding tramp for the next half-hour amidst heather and waving brake-fern, winning our way at last to a fine view point dubbed the Giant's Chair. The outlook hence on a fine summer's day is a thing to be remembered. Wide and varied as is the prospect, the gem of it all, perhaps, is the charming bird's-eye view of old Ludlow town, down in the vale at our feet, its warm-grey towers and house-roofs nestling beneath the verdant slopes of Whitcliff, which in their turn are overtopped by the brindled heights of Bringwood Chase, stretching away towards the blue Welsh hills where the horizon meets the sky.

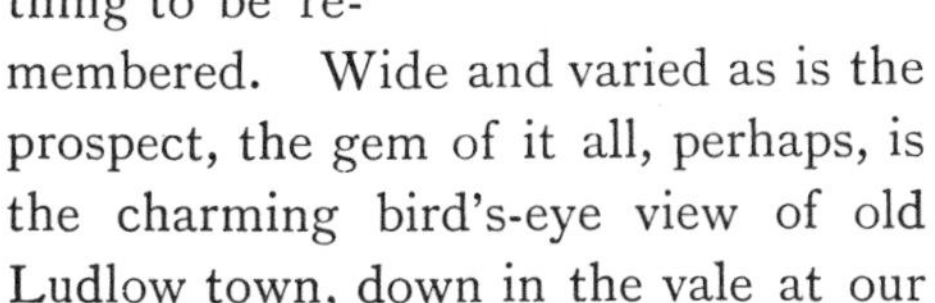

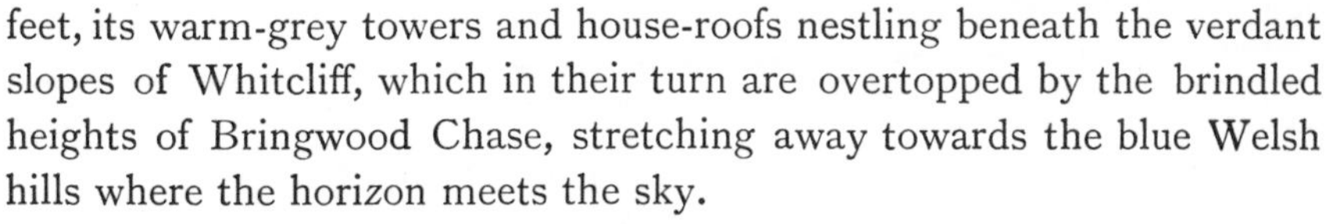

CROW LEASOW

Having spied out the land from this lofty eyrie, we plunge down again through the breast-high bracken, and then, working our way by cross-country lanes, come presently to Crow Leasow.

Crow Leasow is a substantial brick farmhouse dating from the early days of the seventeenth century. Its weatherbeaten front has some good moulded brickwork about the doorway, eaves and gables, and a bulky chimney-stack projects towards the northern end. The massive doors and thick beams and rafters of the interior look quite in character; while a gigantic oak tree, of enormous girth but hollow within, flings its vast limbs athwart the greensward before the entrance way.

In bygone days Crow Leasow belonged to a family of the name of Shepheard, who lived here for five successive generations, and were probably the builders of the existing house.

At Middleton village we find vestiges of a yet more antiquated dwelling, in the moated manor-place called the Brook House, whereof one half-timbered gable still survives. From a map made in 1721, the mansion would appear to have been in good preservation at that time, as the sites of a summer-house, a large walled garden and a bowling-green, are all marked upon it.

Laying a course due west for Stanton Lacy, we have now to negociate some intricate byways athwart Hayton's Bent, a stretch of shaggy upland islanded, so to speak, in Corve Dale. Up through the woodlands we go, getting a fleeting glimpse of Downton Hall, standing in a lonely situation amidst a richly timbered park. Anon we strike into a secluded dingle—one of those 'Hopes,' as they are called, so characteristic of a Shropshire countryside, with a brooklet tinkling along through a tangle of undergrowth; while the carol of thrush, linnet and blackbird sounds blithely in our ears.

Stanton Lacy itself is but a mile farther on; and through that quaint, quiet village lies our way to the parish church. Stanton Lacy church is a genuine Saxon edifice; indeed, it is considered to be one of the best examples of pre-Norman work in this country. Upon its outer walls appear the narrow buttresses built of long-and-short stones, and the rough, uneven stonework with its wavy coursing, that mark the Saxon period.

In the north nave wall is the remarkable doorway shewn in the accompanying sketch. Here we find the long-and-short work both upon the jambs and the semicircular head, which is surmounted by a peculiarly shaped cross, and guttæ, or drops, like those found in classic architecture. Though now blocked up, this doorway is still in a good state of preservation.

The church is cruciform in plan, its massive central tower grouping prettily amidst a setting of verdant foliage, when viewed from the south, with the porch standing prominently out, and some curious stone effigies of the de Lacys under low, cusped, mural arches.

STANTON LACY.

Inside we find traces of various styles and dates, with scraps of ornamentation here and there, such as the alternate shields and rosettes upon the otherwise plain stone font, and the little carved figures that look down from brackets on a beam of the chancel roof.

A pretty legend tells how this church first came into existence. Milburga, the pious daughter of King Penda the Mercian, fleeing one day from the too pressing attentions of a certain Welsh princeling, managed to escape across the Corve, near where the church now stands, before her lover came up. Then the good lady vowed a vow that, if permitted to escape, she would build a church as a thank-offering; whereupon a mighty flood swept down the stream and effectually put a stop to all pursuit; and so it came to pass that the first church arose hard by upon the banks of Corve.

So much, then, for Stanton Lacy church. In other ways, also, the place seems in bygone times to have been of some importance, for Anderson tells us that 'Stanton Lacy was free from hundredal subjection, and its seigneural lords claimed to have a gallows, to hold pleas of bloodshed and hue and cry, and an assize of ale.'

Upon resuming the onward route we traverse a pleasant vale, the road following up the course of the Corve, with low, wooded hills on either hand, and the topmost crests of the Clees peering over their shoulders. Beyond the fine old timbered farmhouse of Langley the valley broadens out, and the good red soil of Corve Dale shews rich and ruddy where the ploughshare has lately passed, and ripening crops by the wayside add a zest to the general outlook.

Anon we steer a due northerly course, with first a conspicuous Lombardy poplar, and then a curious-looking church steeple, by way of guide-marks. The village to which it belongs lies coyly aside from the highway, necessitating a slight détour, and the crossing of a brawling brook.

Thus we come to Culmington, a bucolic-looking village with several good cottages of stone, timber and thatch; and the church, whose spire we have already observed, rising beside the meadows overlooking the Corve. Thitherward, then, let us now direct our steps.

Though somewhat plain, the old church has several good features, and its curiously stunted broach spire is weathered and mildewed to a thousand tints. The rough, plastered walls of the edifice are only relieved by a few slender lancet windows, which are narrower and more sharply pointed than is usual, while one of them looks like what is known as a leper, or low-side, window.

Very plain and simple too is the interior of the church, a dark oak roodscreen alone breaking the monotony of the whitened wall surfaces. A good Decorated canopy with ball-flower enrichment, an aumbry and piscina, some old carved oak pews, and the quaint memorial to a seventeenth-century Rector, are amongst the notabilia that come under our observation.

A hedgeside inn at the end of the village now comes handy for rest and refreshment, both welcome enough to wayfarers who have borne the burden and heat of the day. Then after a sociable smoke and a chat with mine host anent 'the weather and the craps,' we proceed again upon our travels through the byways of Corve Dale.

The road next takes an upward grade, and, approaching the foothills of Wenlock Edge, enters upon a rough, broken country, known in olden times as Siefton Forest.

Anon we quit the main road, and, turning down a narrow lane, presently espy a large, handsome old stone-built mansion of the Tudor period, the ancient manor-house of Elsich. The front towards the road appears to have been considerably renovated, but the rearward aspect is much more antiquated-looking, a projecting half-timbered stair turret, roofed with thick stone slates, rising with charmingly picturesque effect above the last remnants of the moat.

Elsich was during many generations the home of the Baldwyns, who are said to have first settled here in the reign of Richard II. The original house was probably built about the year 1545 by Richard Baldwyn, whose brother William was cupbearer to Queen Mary. Thomas Baldwyn, son of the last named, was committed to the Tower on suspicion of being implicated in a plot to liberate Mary Queen of Scots, and is said to have written the following inscription on the wall while in prison there: THOS · BAUDEWINE · JULIE · 1585 : AS · VIRTUE · MAKETH · LIFE · SO · SIN · CAUSETH · DEATH.

Striking across the fields, we now cut off a corner and look in upon Corfton, where, beside a large tree-covered tumulus, we find a few scanty, very scanty, traces of The Mount chapel, a little old stone building of unknown antiquity, which, though now a mere featureless shell, was still in use, they say, as a place of worship within living memory.

Another mile brings us to Delbury, or Diddlebury, to give the place its full title. Traversing a footbridge where a stream crosses the roadway, we make our way to the church, whose grey old stunted tower rises above the hamlet.

Dedicated to St. Peter, Delbury church is a fascinating spot to the

18

lover of old things, for the fabric bears the stamp of its first Saxon builders, while other hands in later years have added variety of style in pleasingly blended contrast.

DELBURY CHURCH.

A large portion of the north wall, including the base of the tower, is pure Saxon work, built herring-bone wise inside, and of nicely squared masonry without. A blocked doorway shews the long-and-short construction, while high up in the wall is seen a small, semi-headed window, evidently as old as the wall itself. This window bears traces of having had an internal shutter.

The old western tower, as may be gathered from the sketch, is a curious architectural jumble. Owing to superincumbent weight, the original arch of the west doorway has assumed a squat, horseshoe form, and a later but still ancient arch has been inserted beneath it. With its rough, timeworn buttresses, and dilapidated string-courses fringed with moss and splotched with lichens, this old tower looks exceedingly picturesque, and forms a capital subject for a sketch.

Many quaint bits of carved work, both in wood and stone, come to light as we potter about the interior. In the chancel, upon a brass plate under the arch of the Easter Sepulchre, appears an inscription which runs as follows: M · S · CAROLUS · BALDWYN · DE · ELSICH : ARMIGER · HIC · SITUS · EST : OBIJT · 14° · DIE · FEBRUARIJ · AN^{o} · DNI · 1674 : ANNO · ÆTATIS · SUÆ · 77. The Charles Baldwyn here referred to held Stokesay Castle under a long lease from Lord Craven, and his son Samuel was in command of the garrison there at the time of the Civil Wars.

The north chapel here has been, from time immemorial, devoted to the use of the Cornewall family, of Delbury Hall.

Regaining the highroad we get a pretty rearward view of Delbury, the tranquil hamlet with its low grey steeple nestling in a wooded vale, while lofty hills rise away in the background. Thence we push on for Munslow through an orchard country, where the landscape is brightened by the flower-laden trees whose fragrance permeates the air.

A mile short of our destination, the Swan Inn, with its half-timbered gables, its worn stone steps and swinging sign, makes a comely show at the crossways; and presently after we find ourselves at the Crown Hotel, the old Hundred House of Stottesdon, on the outskirts of Munslow village. At The Crown, then, we will outspan awhile, for, situated in the very heart of Corve Dale, the house will suit us 'to a T' as a starting-point while exploring that locality; the more so that, as a rule, the Dale boasts little accommodation above the hedge-alehouse character.

Munslow is a rather scattered village, whose cottages seem to be playing hide-and-seek with one another about a rough, out-cropping hill. As for the church, the place seems at first sight not to possess such an appendage, until, surmounting a steep rocky lane, we presently come upon it down in a secluded nook, embosomed amidst apple orchards, with the comfortable-looking parsonage house peeping out from a grove of trees.

Two or three dark yews and a curious wooden erection, apparently an old lich-gate, lend an air of rusticity to the churchyard. The beautiful old timbered porch shewn in our sketch is the most pleasing feature of the exterior; but the window tracery is worthy of notice,

H.T.T.
THE OLD CHURCH-PORCH
MUNSLOW.

being of excellent though simple character, and original in treatment. The interior of the church has been a good deal renovated, but in one of the nave windows we notice a Virgin and Child in fourteenth-century glass, and a foliated cross cut upon the sill below.

Some later glass in the aisle windows is remarkable for its quaint anagrams and inscriptions, and upon an old slab near by may be seen the following queer effort at rhyme :

A° 1602 :
IN · THE · HOVVER · OF · HIS · POVVER · ONE · DEAD ·
BY · CHRIST · DOE · RISE ·
AND · VVEE · VVHOSE · BOANES · ROT · VNDER · STONES ·
OVR · DVST · HEEL · NOT · DESPISE ·

Some of the original pews in the nave are of massive old moulded oak, with geometrical patterns incised on their ends of earlier character than is usually found in such cases.

Down past the church, from the westward hills, comes a lane that in any but the best of weather must be a mere mountain torrent, paved with the naked rock and overarched by ancient yews. Our way, however, lies through the fields, until, striking the Wenlock road, we diverge to the right, cross the river Corve by a footbridge, and threading our way through deep, sandy lanes, come presently to Tugford. This takes us past Broncroft Castle, a modernized, castellated residence, seated in a curiously out-of-the-way spot for such an imposing pile.

With the ivy wreathing tower and porch, and moss and lichens encrusting its old plastered walls, Tugford church looks thoroughly in keeping with its secluded sylvan situation. Low down outside the chancel walls are certain arched recesses of unknown origin. The small blocked doorway seen in our sketch has a semicircular tympanum, carved in low relief, of evident antiquity ; and a Norman arch with excellent mouldings is found inside the ivied porch. Internally, two curious, grotesque little figures are perched aloft on either side of this door.

Across the west end, hiding a good pointed tower arch, extends the musicians' gallery, where, amidst dusty music scores and other disjecta membra, the old wormeaten band-stand may still be seen. From this same gallery might be heard, until comparatively lately, those mellifluous strains of flute, clarionet, melodion and all sorts of music, wherewith the 'rude forefathers of the hamlet' were wont to wake the slumbering echoes on a Sunday morning; indeed the present rector himself can still recall those 'piping' times.

The very parish bier at Tugford boasts a respectable antiquity, as witnesses the inscription 'Bartholomew Lutley, Anno Dom. 1617,' carved upon it.

From Tugford we climb by rambling footpaths to The Heath, a secluded, upland district, forming a sort of western buttress to the Brown Clee Hill.

THE HEATH CHAPEL.

Emerging from a tangle of plantations, we traverse a few rough pasture fields and soon come to the Heath Chapel, a small, ancient edifice, standing all alone in a green meadow, with sheep browsing

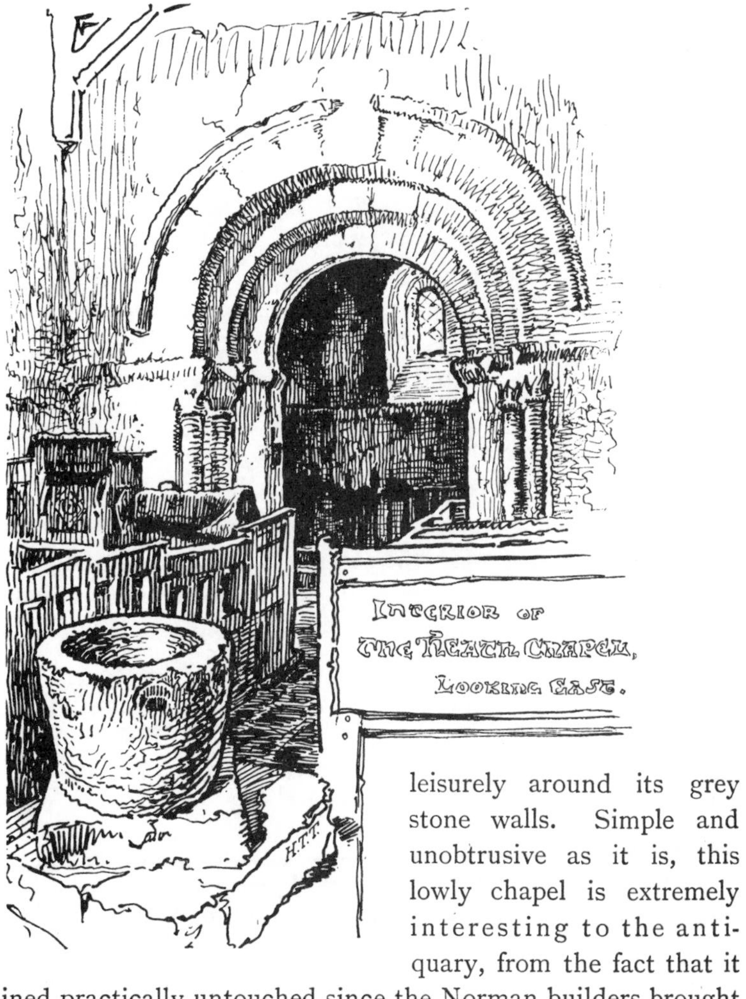

Interior of The Heath Chapel, Looking East.

leisurely around its grey stone walls. Simple and unobtrusive as it is, this lowly chapel is extremely interesting to the antiquary, from the fact that it has remained practically untouched since the Norman builders brought their work to completion, seven hundred years ago.

The fabric consists of nave and chancel, and has a fine south doorway enriched with nook-shafts and chevron mouldings; while the walls are strengthened by the flat buttresses characteristic of that early period, through two of which, curiously enough, the east and west windows have been pierced. A plain string-course runs inside and out around both nave and chancel.

Inside, the old oaken box pews, grey with age, remain in situ, their timeworn panels bearing touches of carved work and quaint iron hinges; the walls retain their coating of faded, mildewy plaster; and the whole wears an air of archaic simplicity, and immemorial repose. Upon the rough stone-flagged floor stands a plain, bowl-shaped font, evidently coeval with the building itself, while the beams of the open-timbered roof look almost equally primitive.

The chancel arch is quite unadorned, save for a little carving upon the capitals. The altar table and rails around, though plain, are not bad specimens of their kind, and inside the western gable is suspended the solitary bell.

As may be readily understood, the congregation here is at the best of times but a scanty one; indeed, it is said that in bygone days the parson, perceiving but 'two or three gathered together,' would sometimes adjourn the service to the snug fireside of a neighbourly farmer's kitchen! The wonder, indeed, is that a church should ever have been erected in such a sparsely-peopled, out-of-the-way locality.

Well, let us now bid farewell to the Heath Chapel, not omitting to notice the old Gothic hinges upon its oaken door, now alas! bereft of that famous key which, if tales be true, was so fearfully and wonderfully constructed that the clerk alone could prevail upon it to 'open sesame!'

The day proving fine and clear lures us onwards towards Brown Clee Hill, whose broad, bulky mass looms prominently, no great distance away to the eastward. In about a mile and 'a bittock,' after passing through a gate, we enter upon a wild, go-as-you-please sort of country, and clamber up the steep grassy vallum of Nordy Bank, a large Roman encampment in an unusually good state of preservation. The bank is very high and steep, with a ditch on its outer side, though much lower, as the custom was, upon its inner face.

Hence a fine, wild glen comes into view, running up into the heart of the hills, Titterstone rears his dark craggy crest away to the right, and the Wrekin peeps over the shoulder of Brown Clee Hill, towards which we now bend our steps.

Dropping to a sandy ford across a stream, we slant gradually away athwart the open furze-clad hillside, and then breast the rough, steep, rock-strewn bank, called Abdon Burf, which encircles the loftier of the twin summits of Brown Clee Hill.

Perched up here beside the cairn, 1,792 feet above sea level, we look down upon every other height in all broad Shropshire; indeed, to find a rival to Brown Clee Hill, we should have to travel across the Welsh border. So let us now turn our attention to the spacious landscape which lies outspread around; a prospect that embraces the greater part of west-central England, and a good cantle of wild Wales to boot.

Away towards the south-east rise the graceful peaks of the Malvern Hills, with the Cotswolds far beyond them. Then to the left are seen the Clent and Lickey heights, and the dingy pall of smoke overhanging the Black Country. Glancing athwart a number of inferior eminences, the eye is arrested by the great rounded dome of the Wrekin, unmistakable in its lonely isolation. League upon league extends the broad plain called Vale Royal, stretching far away into Cheshire, and blurred with a filmy cloud indicating the whereabouts of Shrewsbury:

> 'Far set in fields and woods the town we see
> Spring gallant from the shadows of her smoke.'

The Berwyns come next, a pale grey stripe silhouetted upon the sky-line, followed by the sharp-peaked Breidden Hills, on the farthest confines of Shropshire. Quite near neighbours by comparison seem the Stretton heights, Caer Caradoc, and the spiny Stiperstones; while over those rolling uplands we can faintly discern the topmost crests of Cader Idris, in Wales.

Corve Dale, a chequer-work of ruddy plough lands and varied greensward, lies like a map at our feet, with the rough holts of Wenlock Edge fringing its farther side. Radnor Forest and the Black Mountains extend athwart the south-west, with perhaps a peep of the Brecon Beacons, mere shadows of a shadow these, upon the remotest horizon.

Yonder away lies Ludlow, marked by its tall church tower; and, still following along the sky-line, we descry the abrupt form of the Skyrrid near Abergavenny. Finally our neighbour Titterstone Clee thrusts his rugged cone aloft; a fine, dark, basaltic crag, around whose crest the cloud shadows love to linger; fitting throne for the giant who, in days of old, haunted those lonely heights.

And overarching all this fair landscape spread the 'infinite shining heavens,' and the glorious architecture of the clouds; completing a picture worthy to be stored up in memory's garners for many a day to come.

From the carnedd we make a bee-line down through broad reaches of heather, gorse, and wine-red bilberry shoots, flushing now and then a hawk or a curlew as we tramp along. Hugging the course of a lusty stream, we soon find ourselves once more at Tugford; whence by lanes and field paths we work our way back to Munslow, crossing the Corve at Beam Bridge, where the blacksmith plies his trade in a curious, nondescript structure, half smothered in ivy, built, it is said, as a memorial to some member of the More family who was slain upon foreign soil long, long ago.

* * * * * *

In a retired nook of the hills, about a mile and a half, as the crow flies, from Munslow, lies the old farmhouse of Upper Millichope.

The house is considered by connoisseurs to have been built in the twelfth century, and thus may claim to be the most ancient abode in Shropshire; in point of age, indeed, it probably has few rivals throughout the whole of England.

The oldest, or western, wing of the building, is massively constructed of the grey limestone of the district, its walls being in places at least 6 feet thick, while the steep roof is covered with old moss-clad stone-slates. The original entrance was through the semicircular-headed doorway seen in our sketch, the arch whereof is enriched with ballflower ornament, as is that of a small round window of similar character alongside. The other windows in the lower story are very narrow, mere œilets, or loops such as were used for archery, but are widely splayed within.

Access to the upper regions was obtained by a stone staircase built in the thickness of the wall. This staircase, though now partially destroyed, bears traces of having been protected by no less than three doors between the basement and the room above.

Owing to the reduced thickness of the west wall, the chamber on the first floor is larger than the room below. It is lighted by a pair of double windows in the northern and eastern sides, each window having an attached pillar with moulded cap and base, a projecting socket for inserting a beam across the window, and a stone seat, or bench, in the wall upon either side.

This first-floor room was probably the living-room, or Solar, of the establishment. A small adjacent chamber is supposed to have been used as a chapel, or oratory. In the roof are one or two rickety, dust-laden garrets, long since deserted and given over to mice, spiders, and such-like small deer.

Huge oaken beams support the floor of the Solar, and the internal walls are constructed of wattle-and-dab, now much fallen to decay.

By a 'perambulation,' ratified in 1301, Edward I. declared Upper and Little Millichope disafforested, in common with other places in the same neighbourhood. In those days all this part of the country was a vast tract of woodland, known as the Long Forest; and Millichope was doubtless at that time the manor house, or hunting lodge, of the King's Wood-ward, or Forest-ranger.

Even now the scenery about Wenlock Edge is wild and romantic; but in early times its thickly timbered dales afforded harbourage to robbers and outlaws, who, issuing from the tangled thickets, preyed upon passing travellers as they wandered through its devious, unfrequented trackways. Nor was it until the reign of Henry I. that a good road was made along the Edge, in place of the 'hollow way full of great, sharpe stones, and so narrow as scarcely to admit of two horsemen abreast,' which had formerly existed.

But to resume. From Millichope we may extend our ramble to Rushbury, a pretty village situated in Ape Dale, under the western slope of Wenlock Edge.

Though nowadays so insignificant a place, Rushbury has some claim to be of ancient origin, for it appears probable that the station named Bravinium, on the Roman road from Magna to Wroxeter, stood here, or hereabouts; and it is worthy of note that a hill above the village is to this day called Roman's Banks.

Rushbury church, too, bears traces of high antiquity, some 'herring-bone' work being visible upon the outer walls; while a noble hammer-beam roof, very massively constructed and black with age, lends distinction to the interior, and there are some good oak choir stalls and bench ends, with 'poppy-head' terminations.

Retracing our steps to Corve Dale, we travel on by meadow paths in the direction of Holgate village, whose grey church tower, surrounded by trees, is seen upon a distant hill-top, a landmark to every wayfarer who journeys along the Dale. Wild saffron appears to be the bane of the pasture fields in this locality; but for us they are decked in the purple and gold of orchids and burnished king-cups, affording a charming scheme of colour.

Holgate church is small, and has recently undergone a 'thorough restoration.' It boasts, however, a grand Norman south doorway, enriched by a triple series of arches displaying the boldly carved sculpture peculiar to that period. The font is evidently very ancient, the interlaced ornamentation around the bowl having a Celtic look, while the corners of the base are ornamented with rudely sculptured monsters.

A grove of trees near the eastern end of the churchyard hides a lofty, moated mound; and just beyond that, incorporated with some farm buildings, is a large, circular stone tower, built of good ashlar masonry, and pierced with narrow loopholes of the regulation mediæval type.

Shipton Hall, Shropshire.

This is the only surviving fragment of Holgate castle, founded by Helgot the Norman in William the Conqueror's time. King Henry I., in 1109, honoured Herbert FitzHolgate with a visit; and six years later Richard de Belesme, Lord of Bridgnorth, held his court within these walls. Robert de la Mere, a subsequent owner, died while returning from the Wars of the Crusades.

In the year 1222, one Thomas Mauduit obtained license for a weekly market at Holgate; while the Baron of those days had his own court and private gallows here!

About the middle of the thirteenth century Holgate was alienated to Richard Plantagenet, styled the 'King of the Romans,' by whom it was conveyed to the Knights Templars. Not long afterwards the castle and demesne passed into the possession of Robert Burnell, Bishop of Bath and Wells, and sometime Chancellor of England.

In Leland's 'Itinerary' we read that 'Holgate castle standeth under Cle Hilles, hard by Corve Dale, a 6 miles from Ludlowe'; a sufficiently vague computation, about on a par with others that passed muster in those easy-going times. Holgate castle appears to have fallen into disrepair at an early date, being found utterly dilapidated in 1645.

We now press on to Shipton, not failing to notice the fine Early English hinges upon its south door, as we rest in the porch at Stanton Long church. Approaching Shipton village, the old Hall of the Myttons comes in sight backed by green, wooded heights, making a delightful picture.

As was frequently the case at that period, Shipton Hall follows the plan of the letter E, and is a very dignified example of the builder's art as practised in Good Queen Bess's reign. Between the broad, gabled wings rises a slender stone tower; mullioned windows give back the glitter of the noonday sun, and tall, curiously twisted brick chimneys soar above the roof-tree.

A quaint, old-fashioned garden forms a suitable setting to the mansion, whose silver-grey stone walls and ivied gables rise with charming effect above the flowering plants and creepers that adorn the balustrades in front. Close at hand is an old stone pigeon-cot, covered with a conical roof of thick, mossy stone tiles.

This lordly dwelling was for many generations the ancestral home of the Myttons; having been devised by John Lutwyche to his cousin, Edward Mytton, of Worcester, in the year 1549, previous to which the Manor of Shipton had appertained to Wenlock Priory. The place does not appear to have figured much in local history, but was a veritable treasure-house of heirlooms and antiquities. Times have changed, however, and the tap of the auctioneer's hammer has dispersed these household gods to the four winds.

As befits an abode of 'the quality,' Shipton Hall stands a little apart from the village, with the diminutive parish church nestling under its lee. Thitherward, then, let us now direct our steps.

Shipton church is a building of various dates, and so far has remained untouched by restoration. At its western end rises a weather-boarded bell-turret, while a coating of roughcast of a bright salmon-red tint lends an air of cheerful distinction to the exterior.

A plain Norman chancel arch, having a small arched aperture on each side, gives access to the chancel itself, built, as is recorded in Old English characters on a brass plate let into the wall, in the time of Queen Elizabeth: THIS · CHAUNCELL · WAS · REEDIFIED · AND · BUILDED · OF · NEWE · AT · THE · CHARDGES · OF · IOHN · LUTWICH · OF · LUTWICHE · IN · THE · XXXJ · YEARE · OF · THE · GRACIOUS · REIGNE · OF · QUEENE · ELIZABETH · 1589. The name of Mytton figures upon most of the monumental tablets on these walls. Some scraps of old painted glass may still be discovered in the window above the altar.

A by-lane, running up beside Shipton Hall, brings us in about a mile to Wilderhope, a great, stone-built manor-house of the Tudor period, standing in a secluded spot amidst the woods and pastures of Hope Dale.

Here in days of yore lived a family of the name of Smallman, a race that flourished in this locality during the sixteenth and seventeenth centuries, Major Thomas of that ilk being the hero in a certain episode in connection with a spot called the 'Major's Leap,' whereof more anon.

A spacious stone porch gives access to a large room now used as the farm kitchen, whose ceiling retains some elaborate plaster enrichments, the Tudor rose, portcullis, fleur-de-lys, etc., the letters I · E · S · U on a heart, and certain half-obliterated words, MAL · MEA · DEA · EST, thus they appear to run. Repeated here and there are seen the initials of Francis and Ellen Smallman, who about the year 1601 erected the existing mansion; and a small wainscoted chamber has T · S · I, 1672, cut above its fireplace.

We now hark back to Shipton; noticing a curious sort of grotto, or cavity in the limestone rock, as we pass through the village. Then Corfield is left behind, a place that gives its name to an old Shropshire family; and we get a peep at Larden Hall, an ancient seat of the Mores, pleasantly situated in a well-timbered park under Wenlock Edge.

At Brocton the Feathers Inn affords opportune rest and refreshment; so, after a spell of dolce far niente, we presently strike across country to Great Oxenbold, where in bygone times the Priors of Wenlock had a grange, or residence.

All that remains of the old place is now incorporated with a farmhouse; but the lancet windows of the chapel and the corbel-table above can be detected outside, while a piscina and aumbry, and the brackets that supported the chapel roof, are visible within; besides traces of a circular stone stairway leading down to the cellars, whose ceiling is ribbed with sturdy oaken beams. Evidences, too, are not wanting that a moat formerly surrounded the whole.

Beneath overarching groves and moss-clad rocks lies our way from Brocton to Easthope; ferns and wild-flowers decking the laneside, and rustic children lingering to gather posies, only to throw them aside, as children will, when some new fancy takes them.

Before entering the village, Easthope church is seen, standing in a quiet nook a little aside from the roadway; a small, plain, roughcast structure, of thirteenth century date. From its southern side projects an old stone porch, and a timber bell-cot rises atop of the western gable, all very rustic and simple, and quite innocent as yet of restoration. Upon the porch door still hangs the 'sanctuary' ring; and the interior of the church (which is dedicated to St. Peter) has a very reposeful, old-world air about it, as though time stood still, year in, year out, within these hallowed walls.

The stiff, high-backed pews have a little carved work upon them, with the following inscription: EDWARD · BALL · OF · LONDON · GAVE · THIS · PULPIT · & · PEWES · TO · THIS · PARISHE · WHEARE · HE · WAS · BORNE · IUNE · 28 · ANNO · DOMINI · 1623.

Yonder is the old carved oak pulpit; and upon it hangs the ancient hour-glass, a relic of bygone days. As shewn in our sketch, the hour-

glass is enclosed in a sort of cage, or basket, of wrought and twisted iron, from which projects a banner-like sheet of metal ornamented with nicely fashioned fleurs-de-lys, a heart, and the letters S , S, and surmounted by the figures 1662, indicating the year it was made. Hour-glasses were much in vogue amongst the Covenanters; but although one sometimes meets with the cage, or holder, in country churches, it is rare to find the glass itself in situ as we see it here.

A plain, massive oak roodscreen spans the church, which, besides other antiquated features, has a 'leper' window with fifteenth-century hinge, a bowl-shaped font, and two good Queen Anne chairs in the chancel.

A short mile out of the village stands Lutwyche Hall, the beautiful seat of the Bensons, charmingly situated in an umbrageous nook of the Edge, and surrounded by terraced gardens set about with noble forest trees. Though considerably modernized, the mansion is of ancient origin, as is attested by the date 1587 inscribed upon its front; and there is a rare old plaster ceiling in the entrance hall.

The early British camp on a neighbouring hill was probably an outwork, linking up Caer Caradoc with Nordy Bank.

Setting our faces toward Wenlock, we now follow a high-lying ridgeway road commanding fine views in the direction of the west. Anon we strike into one of the numerous footpaths that zigzag down through the woods, and make for a sort of cave, or rather cranny, high up in the limestone rocks of the Edge, amidst tumbled boulders and brushwood.

This is Ippikin's Rock, the haunt of a robber knight of that ilk, whose deeds were famous in days of yore throughout all this country-side. Here, as the story goes, Ippikin was wont to foregather with his merry men all; issuing forth and levying blackmail on passing travellers, and hiding the stolen treasure in these rocky fastnesses, where the print of the knight's gold chain, it is said, may still be seen. Strange lights, twinkling like Will-o'-the-wisps at dead of night, struck terror into the hearts of the country folk as they gazed in fear and trembling from the rustic homestall, while Ippikin and his crew held high revelry in their unapproachable eyrie.

Eventually Ippikin himself was slain, and his band dispersed, so that they troubled the King's peace no more. But if tales be true his ghost still 'revisits the glimpses of the moon,' and may be summoned from the vasty deep by anyone who cares to stand atop of the cliff at midnight, and cry three times:

> 'Ippikin! Ippikin!
> Keep away with your long chin!'

Footing it merrily along the white ridgeway road, we traverse the watershed of the infant Corve, which babbles away hence towards a place called Bourton. A large old manor-house with a square stone columbarium is the most noticeable object at Bourton; unless, indeed, we except the parish church, a nondescript edifice encompassed by yew trees, overlooking the village upon the north.

Presthope with its limestone quarries is left behind; and then, turning aside near a solitary toll-house, we soon come to a flat-topped rock on the crest of the Edge, known as the 'Major's Leap.' Tradition tells that, in the days of the Civil Wars, Major Smallman of Wilderhope was endeavouring to escape from a troop of Roundheads, when, finding himself hard pressed as he rode along Wenlock Edge, he took a desperate leap from the top of this rock down into the woods below. As luck would have it, a crab-tree broke his fall, though his horse was killed on the spot; and, under cover of the rocks and brushwood that abound hereabouts, the Major made good his escape to his own home at Wilderhope.

Thenceforward, save the goodly outlook upon our left, there is little worthy of note until we draw near to Much Wenlock; and we seek in vain for a certain country inn which greeted the wayfarer in this wise:

'Now Robin Hood is dead and Gone,
Step in and drink with Little John.'

Descending from the uplands, our footsteps echo through the quiet streets of Much Wenlock as we trudge on to our journey's end, while the arrowy swifts are screaming around St. Milburga's tall church-steeple, and the waning daylight flickers slowly away beyond the hills on the western horizon.

·HINGE AT STANTON-LONG·

WENLOCK, WROXETER, AND THE WREKIN.

EATED in a basin-shaped valley, the town of Much Wenlock lies high on the hills, a statement which smacks somewhat of paradox, though the explanation is not far to seek. The fact of the matter is, the place occupies one of those upland vales, locally termed Hopes, so frequently found in this part of Shropshire.

Much Wenlock is a town of very ancient origin, its earliest history centring around the venerable Priory founded by St. Milburga, daughter of Merewald, King of Mercia, towards the close of the seventh century.

Its municipal history, too, dates far away back into the past. Before Henry the Third's time Wenlock already held its weekly market, and in 1468 Edward IV. granted the first charter of incorporation, so that Much Wenlock can justly claim to be one of the most ancient boroughs in the realm. And there is a story, though we know not if it be true, that the very first member who ever entered Parliament was the Member for the Borough of Much Wenlock!

So let us now take a look at the old town, in the centre whereof rises the ancient Guildhall, 'buildid,' as an old record has it, 'over ye Prisonne.' Supported upon massive oak pillars, the upper story consists of timber and plaster, with gables and mullioned windows projecting at intervals, and a deep tiled roof over all. Upon one of these oak pillars you may still see the iron staples of the whipping-post, and under the arches hard by stand the old parish stocks.

Upstairs we find the Court of Assize; the Bench surmounted by the Royal Arms, tempore 1589, and the Sword of Justice. Adjacent is the Council Chamber, a sombre apartment panelled with dark old oak, whose open-timbered roof bears the appropriate legend, JUDICIUM · VERUM · JUDICATE : ET MISERICORDIAM FACITE.

Close at hand rises the parish church, dedicated to St. Milburga, a spacious edifice whose western tower is surmounted by a tall spire, a rather unusual feature in this locality. A fine Norman west doorway, masked by the tower built against it, is only one amongst several good features to be seen here. In the old parish register we find the following interesting record: 'Note that upon the 26 daye of June was service celebrated first in the Englysh tonge, anno primo Elizabethæ, 1559.'

Upon leaving the church we round a corner beside a queer old timbered cottage, and, passing the site of the Bull Ring, come full in view of the tall grey gables of St. Milburga's ruined Priory; while a grim old stone watch tower, now off duty, is seen rising amidst a children's playground.

Wenlock Priory arose from very modest beginnings. Originally a nunnery stood here, presided over by the gracious Saint Milburga, Wenlock's good genius.

Three centuries later—just about a thousand years ago—the Danes overran all this part of Britain, which probably accounts for an ominous blank in the local records about that time.

Earl Leofric, husband of the famous Lady Godiva, rebuilt the ruined church in the days of Edward the Confessor; but the place fell once more to decay, until, as William of Malmesbury relates, Roger de Montgomery took the matter in hand, and, about the year 1071, erected the nucleus of the present edifice.

Of Earl Roger's handiwork, except perhaps the ruined Chapter-house, scarce one stone remains upon another; the slender pillars and pointed arches of the main fabric dating from about the beginning of Henry the Third's reign. The west front is much in ruins, but such features as remain, indicate that it was built during the Early English period.

The Chapter-House & Prior's Lodging
Much-Wenlock.

Entering by the dilapidated west doorway, we see around us, springing from the clover-scented grass, tall fragments of grey stone walls, blotched with weatherstains, and tufted with ivy, gillyflowers and creepers ; while flocks of pigeons flit from point to point, or nestle in the crannies of the masonry. These massive, lofty fragments convey, by their very isolation, a striking impression of the size of the minster, which must have been of cathedral-like proportions, and unsurpassed in the beauty and richness of its architecture.

Indeed, the more closely we examine these beautiful and enduring structures, the greater grows our admiration for the cunning craftsmanship of those old monkish builders :

> 'Firm was their faith, the ancient bands,
> The wise of heart in wood and stone,
> Who reared with stern and trusty hands
> These dark grey towers of days unknown.
> They filled these aisles with many a thought,
> They bade each nook some truth reveal :
> The pillared arch its legend brought,
> A doctrine came with roof and wall.'

Passing through a corner of the south aisle, now the only portion of the church not open to the sky, we enter upon a beautiful sunny courtyard, around whose velvety turf arise the grey, crumbling relics of the Priory buildings.

Yonder upon the greensward appears the Lavabo, or washing-place of the monks ; a circular stone structure, richly carved with subjects from Scriptural history. Beyond it rises the Refectory, an important element in a community which entertained on so lavish a scale ; and farther to the left is seen the picturesque group of buildings that figure in the adjoining sketch.

That long, low edifice, with its quaint, trefoil-headed windows, deep roof and half-timbered turret, is the Prior's Lodging of bygone days ; most interesting in that its internal economy remains much as in mediæval times, though cleverly adapted to the needs of the nineteenth century.

Through those round Norman arches, with their characteristic ornamentation and damaged effigy of St. Peter, we get a glimpse of the ancient Chapter House, roofless now, it is true, but otherwise in tolerable preservation. The walls of this fine apartment are broken up into arcades of interlacing tracery, each tier of semicircular arches being super-posed upon the one below, giving all the effect of an arcade of pointed arches. The work on the southern wall is profusely enriched

with carving, that on the opposite side being plainer, as though it had never been completed.

There is much else to be seen, for, wander where one will about the tranquil enclave, some new beauty is ever revealing itself to the discerning eye; while the sweet, reposeful landscape enfolds the old ruins with its mantle of midsummer verdure. One pictures to one's self this rich and sumptuous monastery in the zenith of its fame and influence, the great Priory church with its crypt and chapter-house, its library, scriptorium, and picturesque Prior's Lodging. One seems to see the sober-liveried brethren plying their peaceful toil in cloister, garden and field, or attending to the crowd of strangers that daily throngs their gates; for whose benefit refectory and kitchen, vivaries, columbarium and well-stocked cellars, yield each and all their tale of good cheer to make glad the heart of man. Then, as nightfall draws on, the long dormitories fill up with wayworn travellers and pilgrims; while those in need of the leech's skill make their way to the hospital hard by.

There are several good timbered houses dotted about the town, notably the one seen upon the left in the annexed view. This formed part of Ashfield Hall, an old abode of the Lawleys, which gave shelter to King Charles after the Battle of Worcester. The house afterwards became the Blue Bridge Inn, and has finally degenerated to a common lodging-house.

In the High Street we notice an old chequered front, relieved by an open balcony, and inscribed: IOHN · AND · MARY · RAYNALDS · 1682. A still older tenement in Shineton Street is said to have been the original gaol-house of Wenlock; though its ancient Gothic doorway and traceried window have anything but a dungeon-like appearance.

Some pleasant spots lie within a measurable distance of Wenlock. Quitting the town by the Broseley road, we glance up at the admirable little wrought-iron sign of the Raven Inn, as we proceed to Barrow. Our way lies past an ancient stone grange, now used as a stable and store-house; and a cottage farther on offers refreshment to the thirsty traveller in the form of 'lemon aid and jingre bier!'

Then Barrow comes in view atop of a gentle rise, its old church tower peering over the straw ricks of a barton; while far away beyond the dark rolling woodlands of Willey Park spreads a rich, champaign country, bounded by pale Midland hills.

Despite its small size, Barrow church proves interesting, having considerable remains of Saxon work both in the chancel and under the tower. This tower is a queer, bulky structure, rising in four diminishing stages, hoary and weedgrown, at the west end of the church; and a rather curious south porch and sundial keep it in countenance.

Out in the churchyard, beneath a flat stone slab, rests all that was mortal of Tom Moody, the famous Whipper-in, who, when his hunting days were ended, was 'run to earth' at this spot in the year of grace 1796. A century ago, Tom Moody's was a name to conjure with in all this countryside; and tradition tells how his sporting comrades, determined to be 'in at the death,' gathered at the grave-side to give their old friend a parting 'view-halloo!'

AN OLD INN-SIGN AT BROSELEY.

Past a group of seventeenth-century Almshouses we travel on to Broseley, home of the Broseley Clays, beloved of fireside smokers. The town, with its mean brick dwellings, has a decayed look about it; but in one of the streets, outside a public-house, we chance upon a rare example of local wrought-iron work, which is illustrated above.

'Fight to the left at the cross-roads, and then you canna miss the way,' remarks a passer-by of whom we now enquire the route to Benthall. Dumpy, pot-bellied pottery kilns, bowered in flowering hawthorn, rise by the roadside, where the brilliant blue Borage is abloom in untended corners.

A fine avenue of forest trees leads us to Benthall Hall, a stately freestone mansion of the sixteenth century, its mullioned windows and projecting porch making a goodly show in the landscape. Close at hand, its only neighbour, appears the parish church, a curious little whitewashed edifice, destroyed and rebuilt at the time of the Great Rebellion, when Benthall was held for the King. Its internal economy is a survival of the churchwarden period, down to the stiff, penitential box-pews, and the faded red curtains in the southward windows.

In olden times an extensive tract of woodland, called the Royal Hay, or Forest, of Shirlot, covered the rough broken country lying to the south of Broseley.

About the centre of this district lies Willey Park, the ancient demesne of the Foresters; an estate which has never, it is said, been bartered for filthy lucre since first it was granted by Henry II. to the Keeper of the Royal Forest.

The Foresters of bygone days seem to have been a free, open-handed race, and keen sportsmen to boot. Tom Moody himself made his name famous amongst the fox-hunting squires and parsons, who rode to hounds in the train of my Lord Forester.

Willey Hall, a solid, substantial stone edifice, stands atop of a gentle rise, overlooking a chain of lake-like pools embosomed amidst shadowy woodlands. Half a mile east, in a nook of the park, lies Willey church; near to which we notice a natural curiosity, an oak and an ash tree enjoying life on the co-operative principle by sharing a single stem between them.

Thenceforward our way lies through a reach of old forest land, full of gnarled timber trees and carpeted with ferns—remains of Shirlot Forest. In the heart of these woodlands we come upon a tall, ruinous stone obelisk, known as the Shirlot Monument; whence, after traversing the gorse-clad uplands of Shirlot Common, we return in due course to Much Wenlock.

* * * * * *

Road and rail keep fast company through Farley Dingle, the deep, picturesque defile, by which one descends from Much Wenlock to the vale of Severn. A brawling stream, as it winds adown the dingle, has been ponded in and set to drive some rustic mills upon its banks.

About half-way down we come to a place called Lawley's, *i.e.* Lawless, Cross; recalling the wild times when outlaws took advantage of the fact that this spot, being on the debatable line between the franchises of Wenlock and Buildwas, formed a sort of No-man's-land, where the arm of the law scarce reached.

Emerging from the hanging woods of Farley Dingle, a broad, fertile valley opens out before us, with the Severn rolling along through rich pasture meads, and the ivy-clad ruins of Buildwas Abbey seated beside its banks. So first for a bit of derivation. 'Build' suggests bieldy, or bield, the Scottish equivalent for sheltered, comfortable; and 'was' is a termination associated with a low, waterside situation, as for example Sugwas, near the river Wye, in Herefordshire.

After the manner of their cloth, those old Cistercian monks, who erected Buildwas Abbey, seem to have had an eye to the picturesque in locating their noble foundation. Rising amidst green, folding meadows, on the right bank of the Severn, the ruined Abbey forms the central feature in a beautiful, tranquil scene; and, set amidst rich, dark foliage, with the river rolling by, and cattle standing knee-deep in the shallows, has exercised the brush of many a landscape artist.

Founded by Roger de Clinton, Bishop of Chester, early in King

Stephen's reign, Buildwas Abbey is built in a plain, severe style, offering a striking contrast to its more elegant rival at Much Wenlock. It was the home of a wealthy community, owning, it is said, no fewer than nine granges in Shropshire alone. A beautiful cope, worked by the hands of Fair Rosamund, the Lady of Clifford Castle, was amongst the most valued chattels appertaining to Buildwas Abbey.

The arrangement of the several buildings is simple enough. East and west extends the great monastic church, fairly intact still, though minus its roof; a cruciform edifice with substantial circular pillars, slightly pointed Transitional arches, and round-headed clerestory windows; while a massive tower of Norman date rises above the crossing. The choir is probably older than the nave, though the triple sedilia, with its pretty dog-tooth enrichment, is evidently not earlier than the thirteenth century.

Towards the north one can trace the cloister-garth, where the Chapter House, with its groined roof and slender, elegantly-proportioned pillars, may still be seen. Beyond this lay the Abbot's dwelling, now a private residence; with its chapel, ambulatory, and noble dining-hall spanned by an open-timbered ceiling. In the vale towards the west lay the vivaries, or fishponds, fed by a stream that runs down from the neighbouring hills.

At Buildwas Abbey, the monks of old kept alive the lamp of civilization in dark, mediæval days. 'Within these walls peace reigned; from their stately chambers ever arose the sound of prayer and praise; their gates were open to the pilgrim and the traveller; hospitality, and brotherly kindness, softened in many ways the harsh incidence of feudal custom.'

Looking down-stream, as we stand upon Buildwas Bridge, we get a glimpse of that dun, smoky district, which, like the black patch on a Court beauty's cheek, seems to heighten by contrast the charms of the fair landscape around.

In the heart of this dingy region stands Madeley Court, a large, rambling old manor-house of late Elizabethan, or perhaps early Jacobean, date. At the time of Domesday Survey, the Manor of Madeley appertained to Wenlock Priory; and in Edward the First's reign the Priors obtained the King's license to enclose a park from the neighbouring Forest of Mount Gilbert.

As may be gathered from our sketch, Madeley Court is an extremely picturesque old pile; the quaint stone gate-house in the foreground, with its turrets and mossy, stone-tiled roofs, contrasting pleasantly with the mellow tints of the ancient mansion beyond.

The scene is, unfortunately, much marred by its grimy environment; and there is little to attract one in the interior of the dwelling, which is

MADELEY COURT.

tenanted by several humble workmen's families. The pool at the rear is a relic of the Prior's fish-ponds, whence a stream ran away to turn the wheel at the Manor Mill hard by.

Beyond the fact that it was used as a country residence by the Priors of Wenlock, but little is known about the history of Madeley Court. The Ferrars family, we believe, made it their home at one time; and in Charles the First's reign the mansion was in the hands of a stout old Royalist, one Sir Basil Brooke.

In the grounds upon the west side of the Court stands a very remarkable sundial, or planetarium, probably as old as the house itself. It consists of a large block of blackened freestone, supported upon a low base, with cup-shaped holes scooped upon three of its sides. Each of these holes originally contained a dial, but the dials themselves have long since disappeared. This curious astronomical instrument, besides being used as a sundial, could, it is said, be also employed to find the position of the moon in relation to the planets.

But to return to Buildwas. After passing the Abbey Hotel, a large, oldfashioned hostelry, well known to brethren of the angle, we have a delightful stroll by Severn side, with the ruins of Buildwas Abbey full in view across the water, and a lowly church peeping out upon the opposite side the way.

Through a country where cornfields and pasture lands alternate pleasantly, we push briskly on into Leighton, a tree-shaded village seated beside a wide horseshoe reach of the Severn. Time out of mind has this noble demesne been an appanage of the knightly family which gives the place its name; indeed, there was already, they say, a de Leighton here when Henry I. came to the throne. The little church, close by the Hall, contains effigies of Sir Richard de Leighton, a fourteenth-century knight arrayed in full battle harness, and of Sir William and his lady, who flourished about a century later.

Life, one would suppose, must be worth the living amidst these quiet, rural scenes; and several of the villagers who rest in the green churchyard have, we observe, well outrun a century ere they could tear themselves away.

Vorwärts! Anon we descry Eaton Constantine, the 'Etune' of Domesday Book, a high-lying village held by Constantine the Norman at the rental of a pair of white gloves, valued at one penny! Richard Baxter, the puritan Divine, spent his early days up there, where his dwelling may still be seen.

Passing by a timber bridge across the Severn, we travel on to Cressage; going near a very old manor-house now known as the Eye, or Island, farm. This pretty village near Severn side derives its Domesday name of Cristes-ache (*i.e.* Christ's-oak) from a tradition that the Gospel was first preached in this locality beneath the shade of an oak tree. This tradition is supported by the fact that a very ancient oak, in the last stages of decay, standing on the outskirts of the village, has from time immemorial been known as the Lady Oak ('Our Lady's Oak'), probably a mediæval perversion of the earlier Saxon name.

Belswardine House, on the hillside overlooking Cressage, is associated with Judge Jeffreys, of execrable memory, who lived there for a time.

Upon regaining the Leighton road we soon come to an elevated spot called Watch Oak, whence we get a rare view over the plain of Shropshire, and the towers and spires of the county-town, with the blue hills of Wales soaring far away beyond the borderland heights.

THE LADY OAK, CRESSAGE.

Eyton village lies only a mile away now, on a hill overlooking the Severn. Eyton claims, we believe, to be the birthplace of that accomplished scholar and author, Lord Herbert of Chirbury. The remains of Eyton Hall are now incorporated with a farmhouse; it was built by Sir Thomas Bromley, one of the executors of King Henry the Eighth's will, and Lord Chancellor of England, in the last year of Edward VI. From the Bromleys the estate subsequently passed, by the marriage of Sir Thomas's heiress, to the Bridgman family.

An obscure, winding lane, brings us in due course to the village of Wroxeter. Here we are on ground classic to the archæologist, for beneath our feet lie the ruins of Roman Uriconium. 'The site of this long-deserted town,' writes Professor Paley, in the *Nineteenth Century* magazine, 'probably the most important one between Dover and Chester (London not even excepted, till the latter days of the Roman occupation), is of great extent, and it must have formed one of the chief places of defence against the turbulent inhabitants of Wales. Probably it was built as a precaution that the extremely strong position of the Wrekin should not be occupied by the enemy.'

Towards the close of the fifth century Uriconium was overwhelmed by the Saxons; when the 'high-placed city of Wrecon,' as Llywarch-Hên, the old Welsh bard, styles it, was utterly destroyed, and reduced to a heap of ruins. In mediæval days these ruins doubtless fell a prey to the pious monkish builder, who was very busy about that period; and, as time still wore on, meadows and cornfields covered the forgotten site, and the countryman wondered to see the coins and curious ornaments turned up by his passing ploughshare.

Thus matters remained until about the middle of the present century; when the Shropshire Antiquarian Society opened up so much of the ruins as funds would allow, though by far the larger portion of the 'English Pompeii' remains to this day a terra incognita. Some fine day, perhaps, this fascinating search will be renewed; for, in its glorious uncertainty, the quest for antiquities is like prospecting for gold, 'You can't tell anything about gold,' a digger once remarked, 'you're just as likely to find it where it ain't as where it are!'

A green mound, running across country in a horseshoe form, marks the limits of ancient Uriconium. Of this wall, the only portion remaining above ground is a large mass measuring about 20 feet in height, by 3 feet or so in thickness, and constructed, as was usual in Roman work, with bonding-courses of thin red tiles, alternating at intervals with the small squared stones of the masonry.

Traces of arches with lateral walls between them are visible upon its southern side; and somewhat farther from the wall, on the south, or 'city' side, may be seen the massive substructure of a building considered to have been the Basilica, or, perhaps, Government Hall, of the town. Close at hand appears an elaborate system of hypocausts and tiled flues that supplied the hot baths, all in a very fair state of preservation. Several skeletons were discovered in this portion of the ruins, besides a number of coins, whose superscriptions gave a clue to the date of the city's destruction. A hut near the entrance contains many interesting objects brought to light in course of the excavations.

But for the finer, more perishable objects found here, we must go to the excellent Museum at Shrewsbury, where one may study at one's leisure the countless articles of household use, personal adornment or what-not, that speak, more eloquently than any description, of the everyday life of Uriconium, sixteen hundred years ago.

The Watling Street, that great military highway of the Romans, passed through the city of Uriconium on its way from London to North Wales. Another Roman road went southwards from the city; running viâ Church Stretton, Leintwardine and Kenchester, to Abergavenny in Monmouthshire.

We now retrace our steps to Wroxeter, and, crossing the line of the ancient fosse, soon come to the parish church. Its tall, picturesque-looking tower is relieved by ornamental string-courses, and small niches with figures in them; while queer, uncouth gargoyles project from the angles, as may be noticed in the sketch.

Wroxeter church was originally a collegiate foundation, with four resident priests, and a chantry dedicated to St. Mary the Virgin. In 1155 William FitzAlan, Lord of Wroxeter, presented the church to the monastery of Haughmond, to which it continued to belong until the Dissolution.

From the Normans onwards, many builders have left their impress upon this fine old fabric. Good Norman windows and a doorway of the same period occupy the south wall of the chancel, where are several table monuments, of which the most interesting, perhaps, is that to Sir Thomas Bromley, whose house we have lately noticed at Eyton, and an elaborate table-tomb, with effigies of Sir Richard Newporte, and Dame Margaret his wife.

An ancient register chest in the vestry has its surface traceried over

THE RUINS OF URICO-NIUM, and WROXETER CHURCH-TOWER.

with elaborate ironwork. The font is curious, being fashioned from a Roman capital; and various architectural odds-and-ends of Roman origin are preserved in a garden adjoining the churchyard. Even the pillars on either side the gateway, seen in our sketch, are treasure-trove from the buried city.

Farewell now to Uriconium, and to Wroxeter, its offspring, with their time-honoured associations. Along the old Watling Street lies our way, until, entering the Salop road, we cross the Bell brook near the site of the Roman wall and trudge on past Attingham, serenely seated amidst its broad demesne, with rich pastures and umbrageous woodlands spreading away on either hand. Traversing Tern Bridge we presently come to Atcham, a trim, well-cared-for-looking village, with a fine old church close by Severn side, a handsome balustraded bridge spanning the broad river, and memories of Ordericus Vitalis, the historian of William the Conqueror, a native of Atcham.

Dedicated to St. Eata, Atcham church is built of a reddish stone, supposed to have been brought from the ruins of Uriconium. It has a seventeenth-century timbered porch, and a fine traceried oak roodscreen, brought, we believe, from Worfield church; while the carved panels of the oak lectern illustrate the parable of the Prodigal Son.

The only monument worthy of note is that of Jocosa Burton, an incised slab brought from Old St. Chad's, Shrewsbury, and dated 1524. In one of the south nave windows we notice some good stained glass representing Blanch Parry, one of Queen Elizabeth's gentlewomen, kneeling at her mistress's feet, with the Parry arms and an inscription recording her death in 1589. This glass was brought from Bacton Church, Herefordshire, where Blanch Parry's fine monument is still to be seen. It was illustrated in 'Nooks and Corners of Herefordshire,' some few years ago.

Crossing the bridge, we obtain a good view of the church reflected in the placid river; and thereafter we stretch away along the Watling Street, Rome's grand Prætorian thoroughfare of days gone by. Presently Uppington and its ruined castle appear upon our left, looking across Tern river to Withington, where the curious church brasses are.

By-and-by we come to Hay Gate, where, as the name suggests, we enter upon the 'Royal Haye of Wellington,' a tract of woodland emparked by the Normans from the Forest of Mount Gilbert. This forest was formerly very extensive, spreading over more than one of the old Domesday Hundreds; and it was not until John's reign that a charter was obtained to disafforest the district.

So now, with the smoke of Wellington lurking upon the rear, we set our faces southwards, where the dark wooded flanks of the Wrekin swell upwards to meet the sky. Geologists tell us the Wrekin is the oldest mountain in England; and, as the typical hill of our county, it has given rise to the time-honoured Salopian toast, 'To All Round the Wrekin.'

ATCHAM.

Folk-lore, too, has had its say anent this famous hill. 'The Devil,' so the story runs, 'had an old spite against Shrewsbury, so he determined to bring a flood upon it; he would stop up the Severn! For this purpose he came with a great spadeful of earth; but, outwitting himself, as many of his children do, he lifted more than he could carry. Presently he became fatigued upon his way to the river, and let some of the mould fall—that is the Ercal (a smaller hill adjoining the larger). Then he upset it all—and that is the Wrekin.'

Beneath the hanging woods of Ercal lies our onward way. After passing Buckatree, *i.e.* Buck-i'-the-Tree, Hall, we traverse a shady dingle, and tackle the climb to the summit of old Wrekin himself; an exhilarating pull beneath whispering fir-trees, and by grassy glades carpeted with soft moss and springy pine needles, glimpses of blue distance between whiles whetting one's appetite for the good things to come. Nor is the scene wanting in animation, the ubiquitous lover and his lass figuring prominently in every prospect; for Wrekin's brow is a favourite haunt of picknickers and holiday folk from all the Midland parts.

From 'Hell's Gate' we ascend to 'Heaven's Gate,' and so win our way to the brow of the Wrekin, 1,335 feet above the sea. 'There is on the Toppe of this Hill a delicate plaine Ground, and in this plaine a fayre Fountaine,' wrote Leland, the antiquary, long ago. No water is to be found there now except such as collects, from time to time, in the 'Raven's Bowl,' a cup-like depression on the top of a conical outcrop of rock, known as the 'Bladder, (or Balder's) Stone.' At the foot of this rock there is a deep, narrow, crooked cleft, yclept the 'Needle's Eye.' Now the fable goes that, if any young maid dips her foot into the Raven's Bowl, and then 'threads the Needle's Eye,' by scrambling through the cloven rock, she will be married within a twelvemonth, 'so sure as there's acherns in Shropshire.'

Owing to an isolated situation, the Wrekin commands a better all-round view than some of his loftier compeers. To merely chronicle a lot of remote hill-tops would, however, convey but a bald impression of a scene which owes so much to atmospheric effect; so we will only remark that the prospect embraces hills so wide asunder as Axe Edge, near Buxton, and the Brecon Beacons in South Wales; Cader Idris, above Dolgelly, and Bardon Hill in Leicestershire—'a delightfully awful prospect,' as someone has quaintly described it.

A goodly cantle of Shropshire lies at our feet, like a map unfurled on a table; its heights and hollows beautifully diversified by cornfields and orchards, verdant pastures and ruddy plough-fields; while in and between the green hedgerows are seen, like the meshes of a huge net.

Towards the east, the landscape is sadly marred by the smoke of the Shropshire coalfield; so we turn to the opposite quarter, where the Wrekin, falling away by Primrose Hill, bathes his feet in the silver Severn. Yonder in the vale we can just descry the ruined Abbey of Buildwas, with Wenlock church-steeple peeping over a neighbouring hill. That high-lying village away to the left is Little Wenlock, 'Wenlock under the Wrekin,' as it was anciently called.

After 'boxing the compass' in a final farewell glance, we bid adieu to the Wrekin, and plunge downhill again by way of 'Hell Gate'—facilis descensus Averni—until by-and-by we come to Wellington, a place that, from the diminutive 'vill' of King John's days, has grown to a smoke-begrimed mining centre, with little attraction for travellers, like ourselves, in search of the picturesque.

But near the Watling Street, about a couple of miles away, we find 'metal more attractive,' in the form of a fine old timbered manor-house, called Arleston. The date 1614, upon one of its gable-ends, is probably not that of the main structure, which looks considerably older.

There are some very fine plaster ceilings inside, with fruit and foliage elaborately interwoven amidst scenes from the chase, etc., and curious plaster pendants. A small painted figure, let into the wall, is said to represent King James I. In olden times Arleston was used as a hunting-box by the Lords Forester; when, no doubt, it was a place of some consequence. It is now occupied as a farmhouse.

THE SIGN OF THE RAVEN
MUCH-WENLOCK.

LILLESHALL ABBEY,
SHROPSHIRE.

TO LILLESHALL ABBEY, TONG, AND BOSCOBEL.

FROM Wellington, a short spin by train brings us to Donnington station. Here we alight, and, running the gauntlet of some grimy ironworks, we strike into a cross-country road and make for Lilleshall Abbey. Anon we espy the graceful ruins, overtopped by a wooded hill, with the stately grey façade of Lilleshall House shewing up well amidst a setting of luxuriant foliage.

Turning across the meadows, we now make the best of our way to the old ruined Abbey. The most striking feature still remaining is the rich, late-Norman portal of the west front, which, with a fragment of one slender, ivy-clad tower, figures prominently in our sketch. A beautiful Norman doorway, with bold chevron ornamentation upon pillars and arch, gives access to the choir, the oldest portion of the edifice. Eastwards extends the church devoted to the monks; westwards, the people's church, built at a later date.

To the south, around a square cloister court, rise the ruins of the monastic buildings, the chapter-house, the parlour, the refectory; and beyond these again lay the large fish-ponds, the dove-cot, etc.

All is now far gone into a state of ruin and decay, over which Nature has spread her mantle of luxuriant ivy; while wind and weather have combined to add their softening touches. Set in the midst of a green, tranquil landscape, 'the world forgetting, by the world forgot,' this venerable pile seems redolent of memories from dim, mediæval days, when life went forward in quite another fashion from these hard-driven, high-pressure times.

From an excellent local handbook by the late C. C. Walker, Esq., we glean the following particulars anent the history of Lilleshall Abbey. 'The Convent of the Monastery of the Blessed Virgin Mary at Lilleshull' was founded, about the middle of the twelfth century, for monks of the Order of St. Augustine; Philip de Belmeis, Lord of Tong, being the first Patron of the monastery.

The establishment received charters from more than one of our Kings, besides gifts and benefactions from many pious donors. Yet, in spite of all these riches, the worthy Abbots had much ado to make both ends meet, so great was the host of needy pilgrims that daily came clamouring at their gates, as they journeyed to and fro along Watling Street.

By-and-by came the Dissolution; when the monastery was abolished, the Abbey lands leased to Sir William Cavendish, and the reversion of the whole demesne sold by Henry VIII. to James Leveson, of Wolverhampton, ancestor of the Dukes of Sutherland, in whose family the estate has continued ever since.

About a mile west of the Abbey ruins, at the foot of an abrupt, rocky hill, whence the place takes its name, stands Lilleshall village, with its ancient parish church. Lilleshall church, as we now see it, dates from the early part of the thirteenth century; having in all probability supplanted an earlier structure, whereof the font, a very old stone vessel carved in a primitive manner, is perhaps the only survival.

In the grounds of the old Hall, a stuccoed, gabled house at the entrance to the village, is a large pool, or lakelet, whose waters formerly served to turn the wheel of the Abbey Mill mentioned in Domesday Record.

Lille's-hill, the Hill of Lilla, the Saxon, stands but a bowshot off from the church. Rising amidst a flattish country, it commands an extensive panorama in the direction of the west; though itself of so modest a height that the bulky obelisk, to some defunct Duke of Sutherland, with which it is crowned, seems quite to dwarf the monticle.

Shiffnal, Shropshire.

Due south, as the crow flies, from Lilleshall Abbey lies Shiffnal, a little old market town, whither we now betake ourselves. Emerging from the mirky Shropshire coalfield, the train runs near the ruins of Malins Lee chapel, a diminutive edifice of early Norman date; and then, passing over a tall viaduct, gives us a bird's-eye view of red-tiled roofs and a ruddy sandstone church, as it enters Shiffnal station. Whether or no owing to the warm, mellow tints of these antique buildings, there is a kind of homely air about this quiet townlet; and its principal inn, the Jerningham Arms, is a model of what a country inn should be; though, like some members of the fair sex, it conceals its real age, being much older than the date 1705, inscribed upon the front, would lead one to suppose.

There are several ancient houses dotted about the town, of which a good coup d'œil is obtained by taking one's stand beneath the big railway arch that spans the High Street, whence our sketch was taken.

Notice the substantial-looking house upon the left, a very old building with an early eighteenth-century brick front, and quaint, glazed turret atop. Beyond it is seen a group of half-timbered gables, with carved bargeboards, brackets and moulded beams; while a smaller house of similar character keeps them in countenance across the way.

St. Andrew's church, a fine, cruciform structure, begun about 1180 A.D., rises beside the Bridgnorth road, on the western flank of the town.

From its southern side projects a wide stone porch, with a curious chamber, called a parvise, above it. Enshrouded by dark yews, and with the old, weatherworn tower soaring overhead, this porch makes an excellent study for the artist's pencil.

Within, the church wears a somewhat sombre air, owing to the rich, subdued colour of its ancient masonry. The nave is covered by a handsome hammer-beam roof; while four lofty, elegant arches span the crossing beneath the central tower. Eastward of the crossing we get a glimpse of the original Norman chancel arch, with a bit of carved work above it; and the tracery of the east window, though simple, strikes us as good in style.

Beneath an arched recess in the north wall of the chancel lies the figure of a tonsured priest, cut in stone, with the following inscription: HERE · LIETH · THE · BODY · OF · THOMAS · FORSTER · SOME · TIME · PRIOR · OF · WOMBRIDGE · WARDEN · OF · TONGUE · & · VICAR · OF · IDSALL · 1526: Idsall, it may be observed, is the olden form of Shiffnal, and Tongue is the modern Tong.

Shiffnal Church

A couple of instances of longevity in connection with this place are too good to be missed. Born at Shiffnal in 1590, William Wakley was buried at Adbaston in 1714, aged 124. Mary Yates, another veteran, lived to the ripe old age of 127 years. She is said to have walked from Shiffnal to London when only seventeen, just after the Great Fire of London, in 1666.

Southward from Shiffnal the infant Worf ripples along through a quiet, agricultural country; with a number of old paper mills strung along its course like beads upon a string, and villages and country seats dotted about on the neighbouring uplands.

Overlooking this pleasant vale rises Brimstree Hill, an admirable view-point within easy strolling distance from Shiffnal. 'Mornin', sirs,' says a carter, giving us the sele of the day, as he stops to breathe his team on the brow of the hill. 'Come to look about yer, like? There's many a one I've seen a-standin' here, same as you be, to look at the country yander. It's bin plaguey whot a-comin' up the bank, but we shanna be long now afore we gets to th' Horseshoe.' So, accepting this pretty broad hint, we drop a coin into friend carter's ready fist, and, turning over an adjacent stile, proceed to spy out the land.

And well worth coming to see it proves, for, though our present elevation is but slight, it gives us an outlook over a lordly landscape. As George Borrow very aptly remarks, 'What a beautiful country is England! People run abroad to see beautiful countries, and leave their own behind unknown, unnoticed, their own, the most beautiful!'

Returning to Shiffnal, we proceed thence towards Tong; traversing a broken, undulating country chequered with woodlands, sandy warrens and cornfields, where the young wheat is shot with the scarlet gleam of the poppies. In yonder meadow haymaking is in full swing, the women's aprons fluttering to the breeze, the high-piled waggon half smothered beneath its big, sweet-scented load, and some labouring men resting under the hedgerow. Rooks are swaying hither and thither in the wind, and clustering about the tops of the tall elms in the foreground—altogether one of those breezy, rural scenes, that David Cox and John Linnel knew so well how to portray.

Presently we traverse a secluded dingle, with regiments of foxgloves standing sentinel along the laneside, and ferns and wildflowers galore draping the glades beyond. Then, approaching our destination, the country opens out, revealing a richly timbered vale where silvery meres meander in long, still, reed-fringed reaches, and swans sail to and fro amidst the water-lilies. Hence we get a charming peep of Tong Castle, a large stone mansion of curiously bizarre architecture,

with an old tree-begirt pigeon-house mirrored in the placid waters of the mere.

The original castle had a venerable history, if we are to credit the following tradition. Once upon a time Hengist, the Saxon, having aided King Vortigern in his wars, was offered by that monarch as much land as an ox-hide would enclose. Thereupon the wily Teuton hit upon the device of cutting an ox-hide into narrow strips, wherewith he enclosed a goodly cantle of land, and upon it built Tong Castle.

TONG CHURCH. FROM THE MEADOWS.

Now Tong Church is seen ahead, crowning the brow of a gentle rise, with the ivy-clad ruins of the ancient 'College and Almose House,' stretching down towards the mere below; a place which, as John Leland tells us, was 'an Auncient Foundation of the Vernons of Haddon in the Peke.'

In 'The Old Curiosity Shop,' Charles Dickens has given us this fascinating glimpse of Tong Church. ' " See—here's the church !" cried the delighted schoolmaster in a low voice ; " and that old building close beside it is the school-house, I'll be sworn." It was a very aged, ghostly place ; the church had been built many hundreds of years ago, and had once had a convent or monastery attached ; for arches in ruins, remains of oriel windows, and fragments of blackened walls, were yet standing ; while other portions of the old building, which had crumbled away and fallen down, were mingled with the churchyard earth, and overgrown with grass.'

'They admired everything — the old grey porch, the mullioned windows, the venerable gravestones dotting the green churchyard, the ancient tower, the very weathercock ; the brown thatched roofs of cottage, barn and homestead, peeping from among the trees ; the stream that rippled by the distant water-mill ; the blue Welsh mountains far away.'

Though perhaps the old church is not now in quite so picturesque a state of decay, this description holds good in the main to-day ; and our sketch may convey some idea of its outward appearance.

Upon stepping within we discern, by the 'dim, religious light' that filters through traceried windows, a venerable interior crowded with sculptured tombs, old gothic screens and curiously carved stall work ; all so richly wrought in alabaster, wood and stone, as to repay the closest examination. The Vernon and Pembrugge tombs, indeed, are considered the finest of their kind in Shropshire, and a detailed description of them would fill a good-sized volume.

A 'leper's' door gives access to the vestry, which contains a library of rare old tomes, stoutly bound in faded parchment; and a wonderful piece of ecclesiastical needlework, wrought by the nuns of Whiteladies, Heaven knows how many years ago.

A TREASURE FROM TONG

Then there is the beautiful Cup, or Chalice, which figures upon this page.

This Cup, which is probably of foreign workmanship, is of silver-gilt, richly chased with delicate, scrolly patterns, and a small leaf ornamentation around the middle part, which has crystal in lieu of glass, and lions' heads upon the three upright supporters. The top is formed as a removable lid, and is surmounted by a small knop; and the base is relieved by scrolls, and boldly emphasized mouldings.

Authorities differ as to the use which this interesting and unique Cup was originally intended to serve; but it has been suggested that it was either a 'ciborium,' to contain the reserved sacrament, or a 'monstrance,' for displaying the sacred wafer. It was presented to Tong church by Lady Eleanor Harries, about 1625, but is supposed to have previously belonged to the old College established here by the Vernons in the fifteenth century.

The Vernon Chantry, or 'Golden Chapel,' as it is called, forms a small but richly ornamented annexe on the south side of the church. It was 'ffounded,' as an inscription attests, by Sir Henry Vernon, in

1515, and contains, in a niche upon its western wall, a curious half-length stone effigy of Sir Arthur Vernon, sometime Warden of Tong College, to whom there is a brass upon the floor. At the opposite end of the chapel is the ancient altar stone, with the five consecrational crosses incised upon it.

Having paid a visit to the Great Bell, one of the 'lions' of Tong, and glanced at the quaint bellringers' 'Laws' set up in the tower, we now bid farewell to Tong church, and, traversing the tranquil village, pause at the lodge-gate of Tong castle to examine the fantastic devices carved upon its stone-work.

SIR ARTHUR VERNON
PRIEST-WARDEN OF TONG

Then, with the sunshine lying broad on copse and meadow, we set forth anew into the country lanes; and soon espy an old sand-stone quarry choked up with nettles and bramble bushes, whence, as one may suppose, the masons drew their stones for the building of Tong church.

By-and-by a secluded lane receives us, a lane so grass-grown and untrodden, that haymakers are busy making hay upon its long green track.

Thence without meeting a soul en route we come presently to Hubbal Grange, or Penderel's Cot, as it is sometimes called; a lonely cottage, with some signs of age about it. Indeed, by all accounts, the place seems to have been little altered since King Charles II., in the guise of Will Jones, the woodman, journeyed hither on his wanderings; and was befriended by Dame Joan Penderel, the mistress of the house, and by 'Trusty Dick,' her son.

From Hubbal Grange we get a direction for Whiteladies. 'It isn't a very gain road for a stranger to find,' says the mistress of the cottage, 'but there's huntin' wickets all the way. Keep along by th'urdles, and follow the rack under th'ood, and you'll find a glatt in the hedge as'll lead you down to the brook, just by a bit of a plank-way.'

So off we set across country, coming after awhile to an ivy-clad ruin, standing in a secluded spot under the lee of a wood. Giving this the go-by for the present, we now traverse the wood and hasten on to Boscobel; leaving upon our left the tree crowned monticle, where Cromwell's troopers entrenched themselves to overawe the neighbourhood.

Hubbal Grange, or Penderel's Cot.

Anon the old Manor-house, or Hunting-lodge, of Boscobel comes in view, with the royal oak in the foreground, and a belt of dark woodlands beyond; a scene ever memorable in English history as the refuge of the unhappy Charles II., after his flight from Worcester field.

Everyone is familiar with the incidents of that romantic drama; how King Charles took to flight, with Cromwell's riders hard upon his heels; how, disguised as Will Jones, a simple peasant man, he wandered through Brewood Forest, with the trusty Penderels to guide the way; how the royal fugitive took up his lodging in the hidie-holes of Boscobel House, until, the hue-and-cry waxing ever more close and keen, the King was at last forced to seek a precarious refuge amidst the branches of the now famous oak, while the faithful Dame Joan 'gathered sticks, and diverted the horsemen from the oak his majesty was in.'

This oak tree, or rather a scion of the same stock, rises in a

BOSCOBEL
HOUSE.

meadow a few hundred yards south from the house, the observed of all observers when tourists come a-sight-seeing to Boscobel. The pros-and-cons of its pedigree have proved a fruitful topic of debate among the learned in forest-lore, and the question is likely to remain sub judice for many a day to come. So having made our salaam to

'King Charles's Oak,' we now repair without more ado to the ancient Manor-house itself.

Opening a green door in the boundary wall, we find ourselves in a quaint, oldfashioned garden, with formal parterres and neatly paved pathways, where, traced in white pebbles, we decipher the half-obliterated legend . . . QUINQUE · FRATRUM · DE · STIRPE · PENDEREL · or some such words as those, and the date 1651. Atop of a raised bank in the corner yonder stands 'the pretty arbour in Boscobel Garden, which grew upon a mount, where his Majesty spent some time of the Lord's day in reading, and commended the place for its retiredness.'

Very picturesque and sequestered the old Manor-house looks as we draw near, with its barns and outbuildings, and goodly array of hay-stacks in the barton. What tales could the old place unfold, were it but endowed with the gift of speech to describe the stirring scenes it has witnessed in days of yore. Deep within that huge chimney-stack was concealed a secret stair, whence, in times of stress, a fugitive could escape from the house through a door disguised beneath the ivy; while the windows above are not windows at all, but mere painted imitations.

DAME PENDEREL

But let us look within. We first enter the 'parlour or music room,' a large apartment with wainscoted walls, and moulded oak beams in the ceiling, and a rather curious black marble chimney-piece. Though considerably modernized, it is a handsome room enough; and upon its walls hang oil portraits of Charles II. and Oliver Cromwell.

Thence we pass on into a small panelled chamber, used by the King as a study, or private oratory. It is draped with faded tapestry, and contains a copy of a remarkable portrait of Dame Penderel, whereby 'hangs a tale.' An old canvas, which for many years had been used as a 'drawer' for a kitchen fireplace, proved, upon being cleaned, to be a portrait of Joan Penderel, mother of the young men who assisted King Charles in his escape. It was probably the work of some local artist, and bears the inscription DAME · PENDERIL · ANNO .

DOM · 1662. A glance at the portrait will shew a countenance full of quiet dignity and character, surmounted by a queer, peaked, gipsy hat, a white coif falling around the face, and the red rose held between thumb and finger. Upon the floor of this chamber stands an ancient coffer, carved with a very quaint representation of the Royal Oak, and the words C · R · BOSCOBEL · 1651. This coffer is depicted at the end of the present chapter.

Upstairs we are shewn the secret closet that opens into the great outside chimney already referred to. Then, clambering to the garret, a trap-door is lifted at the head of the stairs, revealing the dark, narrow hole, into which the unfortunate monarch had to squeeze himself whenever his enemies drew nigh. A short ladder leads down into it; and, when Charles was in hiding here, cheeses were rolled over the spot, so that His Majesty might lurk in security, if not exactly in comfort. Hence a rude stairway, fashioned in the thickness of the wall, communicates with the lower hidie-hole, enabling the refugee to escape outside the house by means of the chimney stair before mentioned.

Bidding farewell to Boscobel, we now retrace our steps to the old ruin beside the wood. Here in the depths of Brewood Forest was founded, in Richard Plantagenet's reign, a Cistercian nunnery, which, on account of the white habit of the nuns, was called Whiteladies; in contradistinction to the Black Ladies of the Benedictine monastery, just across the Staffordshire border.

The establishment appears to have continued, with more or less prosperity, until the date of the Dissolution of the Monasteries; but then John Leland's note of 'Byrwoode, a Priory of White Nunnes, lately suppressid, in the very Marche of Shropshire into Darbyshire,' tells its own tale of surrender and spoliation.

Of the conventual buildings little now remains save the north wall of a chapel of Norman date, with several circular-headed windows, a good Norman doorway with a cusp-like ornamentation around the head, and a large arch opening into a transept, now gone. Such slight fragments of carved work as remain, upon capital or string-course, are refined in character.

Dotted about the greensward are seen a number of ancient headstones, only one of which has any interest for us here. Thus runs the faded epitaph: HERE · LIETH · THE · BODIE · OF · A · FRIENDE · THE · KING · DID · CALL · DAME · JOAN : BUT · NOW · SHE · IS · DECEAST · AND · GONE : ANNO · DOM · 1669 : This is that worthy Dame Joan Penderel who, with her stalwart sons, rendered such yeoman service to Charles II. in time of need; and whose portrait we have lately seen at Boscobel House. A large, rambling, half-timbered mansion, which originally formed part of the monastic building, has long since disappeared, leaving not one stone upon another. It is illustrated in Blount's 'Boscobel.'

AT WHITELADIES.

With sun and wind in our faces we now set out for Albrighton, a fieldpath helping every now and again to cut off a corner of the road, and lending variety to the route.

This summer breeze, sweet from the clover-scented meadows, comes very welcome to way-worn, travel-stained tramps. Nature's green carpet underfoot is damasked with buttercups, great white ox-eye daisies, and many another wildflower; while the hemlock weaves its fairylike fringe along the skirts of the hedgerow. The soaring lark pours down her melody as she climbs the sky, and every copse and spinny resounds with the 'charm' of feathered songsters.

But heaven's artillery now mutters in the distance; the birds soon hush their voices in the woods; vast cumulus clouds arise, and blot out the jolly sunshine; the breeze dies quite away, and the sultry air seems big with coming storm.

Suddenly down plumps the rain, in splashes first, as large as sixpenny-pieces; but anon with a steady downpour that drives one into waterproof gear. The brunt of the battle, however, is not for us; the cloud-wrack and tempest rolling away over the country in confused, towering masses, like an army in full retreat; while shafts of sunlight skirmish athwart the landscape in pursuit of the flying foe.

The rain ceasing as suddenly as it began, we push on along the lonely road; with a little, dry, dusty Sahara under each tree overhanging the pathway, and blue puddles in every wheel-rut, like bits of the sky tumbled out of their places. The woodlands re-echo once more to the pipe of thrush, piefinch and blackbird; and the parched foliage renews its youth in the genial, life-giving moisture.

Meanwhile, as the hedgerows, all a-sparkle with raindrops, go twinkling by, we fall to 'blowing the cool tobacco cloud, and watching the white wreaths pass;' and vowing that, let tarry-at-home folk say what they will, there's no such thing as bad weather!

So we jog merrily onward; now meeting a waggoner loading timber at a farmyard gate, anon passing the time of day with an old country woman tending her cow by the laneside. Nothing much worthy of note is seen until, drawing nigh our destination, we come to a place called Humphreston, where the lane takes a sudden turn.

Here we find a large old timbered farmhouse, with huge oak beams in the ceiling of its roomy kitchen, and carved panelling around some of the better rooms; and doors upstairs that still retain their original wrought iron hinges and wooden thumb-latches. The place must formerly have been surrounded by a moat, for a part of it yet remains, besides a good stone doorway in the adjacent boundary wall—altogether a notable old house, which looks as if it might have had a history. Who knows but what it is named after that Humphrey Penderel, Miller of Whiteladies Mill, whose horse had the honour of carrying, as he declared, 'the price of three kingdoms on his back'?

Thence it is but a mile to The Crown at Albrighton, a fine, upstanding old inn, shewing a ruddy, genial-looking gabled front towards the village street, and boasting withal one of the best bowling-greens in the county. So calling in to test the quality of mine host's ale, half-an-hour slips away in no time as we take our ease in the bar parlour, before starting forth to investigate our new neighbourhood.

Guided by the sound of bells, we soon find our way to Albrighton church, which, overlooking a placid mere, rises beside the highway at the farther end of the village.

Though considerably restored, the church is not devoid of interest, a good rose window in the gable of the north aisle being a noticeable feature, as also are the curious circular openings on either side the belfry windows.

In the chancel, carved in marble, John Talbot of Grafton lies in state beside his lady wife; while Master Leonard Smallpage of Pepperhill has to content himself with a bald stone slab, outside in the chilly

churchyard. But he had a goodly dwelling in his time, as we shall presently see.

A bowshot away towards the north, beyond the lakelike mere, stands a rival church, St. Cuthbert's, the parish church of Donington. On the way thither we turn aside to take a look at St. Cuthbert's well, a perennial spring of water much resorted to in bygone days as a cure for sore eyes.

Donington church, like its neighbour across the water, has been largely renovated in recent times. Its thirteenth-century chancel has some interesting features; a good oak roof, supported upon carved brackets, overarches the nave, and some massive oak pews with enriched panels are to be found in the north aisle.

We now retrace our steps as far as The Crown at Albrighton, and, following a bylane, come presently to Boningale, one of those quiet, out-of-the-way hamlets on the road to nowhere, whither the echoes of

OLD WELL-COVER AT PEPPERHILL

ALBRIGHTON

this eager nineteenth century seem scarce to penetrate, and where one's footfall in the silent street brings the villagers agape to their open doors.

A handful of antiquated cottages and small farmhouses, and a little green churchyard with headstones bowered in roses, are soon left behind. Anon, after passing The Horns, a wayside posting house, we strike into a lane leading to the south, and hark away through some broken country to Pepperhill, a curious old dwelling-house standing all by itself, close upon the Staffordshire border.

Built upon an outcrop of the sandstone rock, the house occupies a commanding position, having probably superseded a structure of considerably greater antiquity. The present edifice, partly constructed of brick, partly of stone, has a mighty chimney stack projecting from its southern end; and now affords a home for several cottagers.

The main building has been tastefully fitted up as a rural residence by Colonel Thorneycroft, of Wolverhampton. A kind of observatory has been formed upon the roof, whence a wide and beautiful prospect is obtained towards the west and south.

In the garden hard by rises the curious stone structure shewn in the sketch on p. 169. For want of a better term, it has been called a Fountain, though amongst the country folk it goes by the name of the 'Pepperbox.' It is hexagonal in plan; of Italian, or classic, design; much worn and weathered by time, as well as damaged by careless hands; and appears to be of early seventeenth-century date. Broken, weed-grown and neglected, this old Fountain is so nicely proportioned and finely wrought, that it looks picturesque in its decay. The well to which it originally served as a cover has long since ceased to exist.

Pepperhill, we understand, was formerly an appanage of the Earls of Shrewsbury and Talbot; and was afterwards the home of Leonard Smallpage, whose name we have already seen in Albrighton churchyard. Some scanty remains of ecclesiastical buildings are traceable at Lower Pepperhill, but of their history very little is known.

.THE ROYAL OAK.

BRIDGNORTH

ROUND ABOUT BRIDGNORTH.

CLINGING limpet-like upon the crest and shoulders of a steep, sandstone crag, on the western bank of the Severn, the ancient town of Bridgnorth occupies a situation of more than ordinary picturesqueness. 'Where Severne runneth, Nature hath made a terrible Dike,' wrote John Leland anent Bridgnorth in the days of Henry VIII.; and to this 'terrible Dike' the town owes its unique aspect among all the towns of Shropshire.

Confronting the river rise, tier above tier, the little old brown-roofed dwellings; so closely packed that the cottager, as he stands in his rustic porch, can almost peep down his neighbour's chimney and see what is cooking for dinner! Bits of garden ground with their varied greenery lend a pleasant, rural air; while in and between wind steep, narrow, stepped paths; reminding one of Clovelly, and of certain mountain townlets in northern Italy.

At the foot of the hill, the Severn is spanned by the old stone Bridge whence the town derives its name. Beyond this bridge lies the riverside suburb of Lower Town, occupying a sort of amphitheatre enclosed by the rocky ridge which flanks the vale upon its eastern side.

To see Bridgnorth at its best, let the visitor stand, about sundown of an early autumn day, upon this old bridge; or, better still, take a boat on the river. Then the old town may be trusted to give one a touch of its quality; its brown walls and roofage blending with the ruddy rock into deep, harmonious tints; a ray of light from some cottage pane here and there reflected in the dark, silent water; while the two tall church towers on the crest of the ridge still glow in the last warm rays of the departing day.

So much, then, for general effect; let us now get to closer quarters. Turning our backs upon the Bridge, we bear to the right and enter the

EXCEPT · THE · LORD · BVILD THE H
OWSE · THE · LABOVRERS · THERE · OF
EVAIL · NOT · ERECTED BY · R · FOR 1580

Cartway, in olden times the one and only route by which vehicles could ascend to the Upper Town.

Confronting us as we climb the steep, crooked lane, rises the old half-timbered mansion which figures in the accompanying sketch; one of the few of its kind that have survived the ravages of the Civil Wars.

Built in the sixteenth century, its weatherbeaten front shews the delightful irregularity so often seen in structures of that period.

The interior, half workshop, half mean tenement, has lost all interest for the antiquary, the only indigenous feature being a ponderous lintel stone carved with the ensuing inscription: EXCEPT · THE · LORD · BVILD · THE · OWSE · THE · LABOVRERS · THERE · OF · EVAIL · NOT · ERECTED · BY · R · FOR* 1580. The latter part of the sentence is a cryptic rendering of the name of Richard Forester, secretary to Bishop Bonner, an ancestor of the family which for generations past has dwelt at Willey Hall.

But the name most associated with this ancient residence is that of Dr. Percy, sometime Bishop of Dromore, who was born beneath its roof in 1728. In his day and generation, Bishop Percy was an author and antiquary of no mean calibre; and his 'Reliques of Antient English Poetry' was once widely celebrated.

Mounting upwards again, we pass a group of queer cottages and shops, oddly mixed up amidst the native rock with which they are incorporated; and finally we emerge upon an ample greensward, with St. Leonard's church rising in the middle.

This church has undergone some remarkable vicissitudes. John Leland, in 1536, found it a 'very fayre one'; but during the Civil Wars it suffered much damage through an encounter which took place, between Royalists and Roundheads, in the churchyard; when Colonel Billingsley, commander of the town regiment, was slain.

But of late years St. Leonard's has been admirably restored, and is now worthy of the ancient town it adorns. The original church was mainly of thirteenth-century date; though its noble tower, built of salmon-red sandstone, is of somewhat later style, and rich and handsome to a degree. A fine, open-timbered roof was brought to light during restoration; and the east window has been filled with stained glass in memory of the late Dr. Rowley, who, as Head Master, was for many years the 'bright particular star' of Bridgnorth School. Colonel Billingsley's sword is preserved in the south aisle, where there are also some curious old cast-iron memorial tablets.

In one corner of the churchyard stand Palmer's Almshouses, a series of low, timbered structures, grouped around a small courtyard approached through a modernized archway. This charity owes its inception to Francis Palmer, nephew of Colonel Billingsley, by whom it was established in 1687 for the benefit of ten poor widows.

Close at hand rise the plain, brown brick gables of the erstwhile Grammar School, established in Henry the Eighth's time; a sedate-looking, antiquated edifice, attractive by its very simplicity. A diminutive black-and-white cottage, whose latticed casements look out demurely upon the churchyard, was once the home of Richard Baxter, the divine, ere his name had become famous in the land.

We now pass on into the High Street, a broad, cheerful thoroughfare, over whose uneasy, cobble-stone pavement, we make our penitential progress. Midway adown the street rises the ancient Town Hall, the centre and focus of Bridgnorth, its plain rounded archways bestriding the horse-road, and affording a passage way. Overhead, its half-timbered gable is relieved by oriel windows filled with stained glass; while the steep, tiled roof is surmounted by a slender bell-turret, terminating in a weather vane.

This notable old building dates from the year 1652, having been erected by the burgesses to replace an earlier Town Hall, destroyed during the Civil Wars. Here may be seen the Council Chamber, the Court of Justice, etc., where the town magnates sit in conclave to administer the affairs of this historic Borough; and the modern stained glass windows of the various courts, inserted as a memorial of the Queen's Jubilee, afford a study in the corporate life of Bridgnorth.

Confronting the Town Hall, across the way, appears the ancient many-windowed façade of the Swan Inn, a rare specimen of a country-town hostelry of the spacious Tudor times; and scarcely less effective, though more modernized, are the chequered gables and quaintly carved brackets of a neighbouring residence. The North Gate, last survivor of Bridgnorth's town gates, spans the end of the street with its three uneven archways.

Saturday is market-day at Bridgnorth, as it has been from time

MARKET PLACE, BRIDGNORTH.

immemorial. The long ranks of tented booths, with the crowds frequenting them, make an animated scene; for the countryfolk foregather then from long distances around, and hearty Shropshire greetings are heard on every hand. As nightfall wears on the fun waxes faster; and lucky the housewives whose menfolk win their way home at last in no worse plight than 'market-peart,' to use the Shropshire phrase.

We now push on to Castle Hill, the southern horn of the monticle on which Bridgnorth is located. Before us rises the tall, classic tower

MARKET DAY AT BRIDGNORTH.

of St. Mary Magdalene's church, which, though designed by Telford, the celebrated engineer, already shews signs of instability. Despite its quasi-classic garb, this church is one of the oldest ecclesiastical foundations in the town; having been transferred to Bridgnorth, from St. Mary Magdalene's at Quatford, by Earl Robert de Belesme, when he built Bridgnorth Castle. So old, indeed, is this foundation, that, even in Leland's time, the church appears to have been in a state of disrepair; that painstaking chronicler recording, 'there is a college church of St. Mary Magdalene within the Castle; the church itself is now a rude thinge.'

In the reign of Edward III., William of Wykeham, the famous Bishop of Winchester, held for a time the Prebend of Alveley in St. Mary's church, which was the head of an ecclesiastical district bearing the imposing title of 'The Royal Peculiar and Exempt Jurisdiction of the Deanery of Bridgnorth.'

A stone's-throw farther on we enter the Public Gardens, where, 'all on one side, like Bridgnorth Election,' rises the ancient Leaning Tower, sole remains of Bridgnorth Castle, in its time one of the strongest and most important fortresses in all Shropshire. For some two centuries and a half has this massive, grey, limestone ruin, braved the wear-and-tear of the elements, after Cromwell's men had tried in vain to raze it to the ground.

Built by Earl Robert de Belesme, about the year 1100, Bridgnorth Castle has experienced a chequered and eventful career. Scarcely was the fabric completed, when the rebellious Earl was besieged by Henry I., who, having made himself master of the stronghold, converted it into a royal residence.

Later on came the Second Henry, with Thomas à Beket in his train, and, while investing the castle, had a narrow escape of losing his life by an arrow shot from the wall. In the fourth year of his reign, Henry II. granted to the town its first Royal charter, which has been renewed and amplified by several subsequent sovereigns.

The Castle having been strengthened, and put into a state of defence against 'that great magician, damnable Glendower,' the armies of Henry IV. assembled at Bridgnorth on the eve of the Battle of Shrewsbury, as is recorded in Shakespeare's lines:

> 'On Thursday we ourselves will march; our meeting
> Is Bridgenorth: and, Harry, you shall march
> Through Gloucestershire; by which account,
> Our business valued, some twelve days hence
> Our general forces at Bridgenorth shall meet.'

After a period of comparative tranquillity, Bridgnorth and its castle became involved in the great struggle between Royalist and Roundhead; when the old town showed itself trusty to the core, and true to its loyal motto, FIDELITAS · URBIS · SALUS · REGIS. King Charles I. honoured the borough with several visits; and his rival, the 'arch-Rebell,' was within an ace of being picked off by a marksman upon the castle walls, while riding near to view the defences of the town.

After a stubborn siege, Bridgnorth finally passed into the hands of the Parliamentarian forces, on March 31, 1646. Taking warning by the tough resistance they had encountered, the Roundheads did their best to render further resistance impossible by dismantling and demolishing the castle; and how effectually they succeeded in doing so is attested by the battered fragment we see before us.

Says Leland, chronicling the results of his observations: 'This Castle standeth on the south Part of the Towne, and is fortified by East with the profound Valley, instead of a Ditch. The Walles of it be of a great Height. There were two or three strong Wardes in the castle, that nowe goe totally to ruine. I count the Castle to be more in Compasse than the third part of the Towne. There is one mighty gate by north in it, now stopped up; and a little Posterne made of force thereby through the wall, to enter into the castle. The castle ground, and especially the base-court, hath now many dwellinge Houses of tymbre in it, newly erected.'

From the adjacent gardens, we obtain an excellent survey of Bridgnorth and its pleasant environs; a land of smiling meadows, groves and orchards, encompassed by gently undulating hills:

'Such an up-and-down
Of verdure, nothing too much up nor down.
A ripple of land, such little hills the sky
Can stoop to tenderly, and the wheat-fields climb.'

Yonder is Pampudding Hill, the site of a castle built by Ethelfleda, daughter of Alfred the Great, well-nigh a thousand years ago. Beyond it lies the hamlet of Oldbury, the 'Old-Borough'; a place which, as its name suggests, is older than Bridgnorth itself.

Then there is the winding Severn, spanned by its grey stone bridge; and the ancient town clinging to its rocky hold, backed by ruddy heights and feathery foliage where Apley Park closes in the view.

So now let us push our explorations farther afield. Proceeding along the terraced Castle Walk, we descend the Stoneway Steps, and, crossing the bridge, pass the site of the defunct Hospital of St. John, founded in the reign of Richard I. A little farther on we come to an old gabled house standing in an elbow of the road, and known as Cann Hall. In former times, Cann Hall was the town residence of the Apley family, and upon one occasion Prince Rupert found here a hiding-place from his enemies.

Beyond Cann Hall we follow the Wolverhampton road, which, ascending between high, rocky banks, brings us in a short half-mile to a point where the low, red sandstone cliff has been fashioned into a number of irregular chambers, known from time immemorial as The Hermitage.

'In Morfe Forrest,' writes John Leland, 'King Athelston's Brother lead, in a Rocke, for a tyme an Heremite's life.' Prince Ethelwald, who is here referred to, was the first recorded tenant of this Hermitage, about the middle of the tenth century. In 1335, Edmund de la Mare was presented to the Hermitage of 'Athelardeston'; and, eleven years later, Roger Burghton was 'presented to the Hermitage above the High Road near Bridgenorth.'

Time and neglect have played sad havoc with these singular grottoes, but their main features are still in a measure discernible. The 'Chapel,' an oblong chamber hewn in the living rock, is now partially open to the sky, though the 'chancel,' with its rudimentary rounded arch, remains intact; and there is a shallow, round-topped recess in the eastern wall, where the reredos usually stands.

Alongside the chapel we find the Hermitage proper, a low, dark cell, communicating with it by a small aperture, now blocked by the large, ungainly brick oven, which defaces the interior of the chapel.

There is an apocryphal tale that a passage formerly existed, connecting this Hermitage with Bridgnorth Castle; and that chests full of priceless treasure lay hidden away somewhere amidst the recesses of

COTTAGE IN THE ROCK, BRIDGNORTH.

the rocks; but, needless to say, no treasure-trove has ever been brought to light.

A few paces distant stands a lowly cottage dwelling, which, excavated like its neighbours from the solid rock, was until recently tenanted by a family of modern troglodytes, and is still used in the daytime by the good woman who has charge of the Hermitage. So let us glance within as we pass.

Upon entering we find ourselves in the living room, whose roof, walls and floor, consist of the native sandstone; a warm, weatherproof covering, though blotched and variegated with many a mottled stain. A short step-ladder gives access to a small upper chamber, with seats roughly cut in its rocky walls, and a window pierced through the outer one.

A few hundred paces beyond the cottage there is a large projecting rock, which, for some reason unknown, goes by the name of the Queen's Parlour.

Upon taking to the road once more we soon quit the highway, and, following an unfrequented sandy lane, drop to a secluded nook where the river Worf meanders past a small, ivyclad water-wheel house, with the green glades about Davenport House feathering the hill slope before us.

Through the park we stroll onwards, amidst dappled sunshine and shadow; the rabbits dashing to right and left as we crush through the wholesome-scented bracken, and a nuthatch plying his sturdy beak (like the lusty woodman he is) on the branch of a neighbouring elm. A glimpse of Davenport House, a substantial eighteenth-century brick mansion, and anon we descend the hill past an old circular dovecot, and enter Worfield village.

A pretty perspective of rustic dwellings, each with its narrow strip of garden aglow with oldfashioned flowers, flanks the quiet thoroughfare along which we take our way. This brings us to St. Peter's church, a beautiful edifice whose tall, slender spire is seen soaring far aloft above the cottage roofs as we draw near.

Anent this church there is a legend which runs as follows. The

old monks, it seems, intended to erect their church on the top of the neighbouring hill, so that its lofty steeple might be seen from afar, pointing the way to heaven. But they had reckoned without their host, for, built they never so fast each day, the old Enemy set to work at night and removed every stone to the bottom of the hill, where the church stands to this day.

Be that as it may, we will now take a closer look at Worfield church. To the right upon entering the churchyard appears an ancient, many-gabled old manor-house, with timber-and-plaster walls, and chimney stacks planted askew upon its stone-tiled roofs. Of its earlier history we can say nothing, but in recent times the old place has been put into a state of much needed repair, and converted to the uses of a parsonage house.

Passing a great yew tree, shaped like an extinguisher, we have the church full in view before us; a large fabric of warm red sandstone, whose diverse styles of architecture lend variety to its appearance. At the west end rises a fine tower of three stages, surmounted by the lofty spire, which, some 200 feet in height, has scarce a rival in Shropshire. Several good geometrical windows embellish the aisles, and a porch of similar character projects upon the south.

By this porch we now enter the church; not failing to notice the exhortation, BEE · SURE · AS · YOU · REMEMBER · THE · POOR: 1683, inscribed upon the wooden alms-box near at hand. Curiously enough, the floor of the nave has a downward slope towards the chancel, thus reversing the usual order of things.

A tall, richly carved and traceried roodscreen, divides nave from chancel, which has a plain sedilia and piscina. In the north aisle we notice two admirable, canopied marble monuments, to the Bromleys, and a fine old muniment chest covered with scrolly ironwork.

In the thirteenth century, a certain Henry de Wengham, besides being Rector of Worfield, Alveley, Kirkham and Preston, was Bishop of London, Dean of St. Martin's, and ditto of Tettenhall; a notable instance of pluralism.

Two miles due north of Worfield lies the village of Badger, best known for its celebrated Dingle, a deep, rocky, richly wooded ravine, down which a small tributary makes its way to the Worf. In Badger church are to be seen some well executed monuments to the Cheneys and the Brownes, by Flaxman, Chantrey and others. Isaac Hawkins Browne was a poetaster of some little celebrity in the last century.

Beckbury, with its fine parish church, dedicated to St. Milburga, lies away up the vale of Worf. From Badger we make our way to Chesterton, where are the remains of a prehistoric encampment, half surrounded by the Stretford brook. From these names, and other local circumstances, it appears probable the Romans had a station here-

abouts. There are traces, in some neighbouring cottages, of what looks like a desecrated fifteenth-century chapel.

Proceeding on our travels, we traverse Rudge Heath; and presently after come to Ludstone, a stately old moated manor-house, built by one of the Whitmores about the year 1607, probably on the site of an earlier house.

It is a charming abode, well preserved, yet not over-restored; its Jacobean gables and balconies wreathed in ivy and Virginian creeper; and its antique, pleasantly formal gardens encircled by the moat, where amidst the waterlilies we get an inverted replica of the old mansion.

Passing near Danford, or Daneford,—a suggestive name—we descend a lane hewn deep in the sandstone rock, cross a bridge over a stream, and so win on to Claverley, 'quite a place,' as our American cousins say, and the largest village in this part of the county.

Midway along the street we come to the parish church, a spacious sandstone structure of various periods, crowned by a tall embattled tower. Unlike its neighbour at Worfield, Claverley church remains entirely innocent of restoration, and, from the antiquarian point of view, contrasts favourably with that somewhat spick-and-span edifice.

Overlooking the churchyard, where the gravestones crowd 'thick as Autumnal leaves in Vallombrosa,' rises the remarkably fine old half-timbered house seen in profile in our sketch. This is doubtless the subject of an ancient deed whereby, in 1659, one Richard Dovey bequeathed certain tenements, 'over and adjoining to the churchyard Gates,' on condition that a poor man be paid 'for waking sleepers in church, and driving out Doggs during divine serviss.' The office has lapsed; but whether on account of the rousing character of the sermons in these latter days, history recordeth not.

Close beside the churchyard path, we notice the broken fragments of an ancient stone cross. This cross formerly stood in the centre of the village, and probably dates from about the time of Edward III. It is supposed to have been put up to commemorate the plague, called the Black Death, in the fourteenth century.

What with its lofty, whitewashed walls, its plastered ceilings and high-backed box-pews, the interior of Claverley church recalls the Groote-kerk of some Dutch provincial town; the resemblance being heightened by the peculiar arrangement of the pews, which, turning their backs upon the east-end, face towards the pulpit in the nave.

This pulpit is, perhaps, the most striking object in the church. It is a large structure of the 'three-decker' type, overhung by a great sounding-board terminating in elaborate pinnacles. High overhead stretches a fine oak-panelled roof, partially disguised beneath the ubiquitous whitewash, and adorned with the royal arms.

There are some quaint carvings upon the capitals of the pillars; the Norman front is enriched with arcading and sculpture; and the curious tracery of the chancel windows should by no means be overlooked.

The south, or Gatacre, chapel, contains a lordly alabaster tomb, with effigies of Sir Robert Broke and his two wives. A native of Claverley, Sir Robert was Speaker of the Commons, and Lord Chief Justice of Common Pleas under Queen Mary; departing this life in the first year of Queen Elizabeth's reign. Upon the adjacent wall there are two large marble slabs, with quaint figures in 'graffito,' and inscriptions to the Gatacres bearing dates in the sixteenth century.

But the waning daylight warns us to depart. So, setting our faces westwards, we bowl along between the dusky hedgerows, until we strike the main road near a place called the 'Wheel of Worvell.' Here we linger awhile at the open door of the smithy, whose ruddy gleam of firelight, dancing sparks, and cheerful noise of hammering, attract one irresistibly, awakening some slumbering instinct of the primæval man.

Then putting on the best pace, we spin away along an up-and-down, switchback sort of road, re-cross the bridge over the Severn, and, availing ourselves of the 'Lift,' or Castle Hill Railway, we ascend swiftly and smoothly to our night's quarters in the 'Faithful' town.

This time-honoured Borough of Bridgnorth boasts a number of ancient charters, the earliest of which is the charter of incorporation granted by King Henry II. in 1157. The handsome regalia comprises a pair of silver-gilt maces, a marshall's staff, and a corporate seal; and, last but not least, a modern Mayoral chain bearing the names of the Mayors, the Borough Arms, and the Town motto, FIDELITAS · URBIS · SALUS · REGIS.

* * * * * *

A row up the Severn to Apley Park, one of the pleasantest excursions in this locality, introduces the visitor in a leisurely fashion to the green, placid landscapes, characteristic of 'gentle Severn's sedgy banks.'

Drawing clear of the town, we get a good rearward view of Bridgnorth, perched on its rocky eyrie; and then we pass beneath Pendlestone Rock, whose towering crags are draped in luxuriant foliage down to the water's edge. Hoard's Park and Severn Hall, two ancient timbered houses, are presently left behind, though not in sight from the river; and then, skirting the demesne of Stanley, we come by-and-by to a landing-place at a cool, shady nook, on the eastern bank of the Severn.

Winding upwards through the woods, the steep path lands the wayfarer at a spot where a queer little cottage, excavated in the rock, gives upon a kind of platform, whence one may enjoy a widespreading view over hill and dale and winding river.

Another short climb brings us to Apley Terrace, a charming sylvan drive, which, traversing the crest of a richly timbered upland, introduces one to a changing panorama of almost unrivalled loveliness. If 'to see is to possess,' as Béranger affirms, we have here indeed acquired a goodly heritage. Far beneath our feet, the Severn winds through the vale in a long, silvery reach, embracing the rich rolling woodlands and smooth, green, grassy glades of Apley Park; a worthy setting to the old grey mansion, seated so serenely in its midst. Away and beyond spreads a mazy landscape, chequered with cornfields and woodlands, all mellowed by the touch of Autumn; while our old friends, the Wrekin and the twin-crested Clees, look over the shoulders of their lowlier brethren. Nor is this all, for, by turning across the drive, we get a peep at the Malvern Hills; and Clent and Lickey are seen, rising clear and distinct against the mirky haze that overhangs the Black Country.

In Henry the Third's time, the Manor of Apley was held by a family owning the euphonious name of Huggeford; passing subsequently by marriage to Sir Thomas Lucy, of Charlecote, in Warwickshire. By him the estate was sold, in 1551, to one of the Whitmores of Aston, Claverley, an influential family, who remained masters of Apley during some three centuries or more. For 238 years, it is said, the Whitmores represented the Borough of Bridgnorth in Parliament; a circumstance which gave rise to the well-known local adage, 'like Bridgnorth election, all on one side.'

From the Terrace, here, as we look towards the east, a large farmhouse is seen, standing by itself amidst a grove of trees. This is Ewdness, a fine old brick-and-stone, oak panelled residence of the Tudor period, deriving its name from the ancient family of d'Eudinas, mentioned in Domesday Chronicle. Walter d'Eudinas, in 1221, held the estate direct from the King. Long afterwards it passed into the hands of a Mr. Fletcher, by whom the existing mansion was erected. Fletcher's daughter espoused Colonel Berkeley, sometime M.P. for Shrewsbury, who commanded a troop of horse in the Parliamentary wars. Ewdness now forms part of the Apley estate.

Near Ewdness lived, once upon a time, a damsel named Sally Hoggins, daughter of a local market-gardener. Growing aweary of her patronymic, Miss Hoggins played her matrimonial cards to such purpose, that she lived to style herself Sarah, Marchioness of Exeter.

Beyond Ewdness lies Stockton village, with its interesting Norman church, dedicated to St. Chad. Half-a-mile farther on, on the Shiffnal road, is the hamlet of Norton, where, opposite the Hundred House Inn, beneath a big elm tree, stand the ancient stocks and whipping-post, which our artist has drawn for us at the end of the present chapter.

In Edward the Third's reign, it will be remembered, the Commons petitioned the King to establish stocks in every village in the realm.

Taking a giant's-stride across the Severn, we come to Astley Abbots, a secluded village composed of about half a score cottages, and pleasant, rural residences of the gentry-folk.

St. Calixtus's church, rising a short distance west of the village, is our next objective; an unobtrusive edifice, topped by a small wooden steeple above its western gable. Founded in 1138, it is of the Norman and Decorated styles, and has been reasonably renovated in modern times. The chancel, rebuilt in 1633, has a little painted glass in its eastern window; and the Norman font and richly carved Jacobean pulpit are worth a passing glance. Suspended in a corner of the north aisle we notice a 'Lover's Garland,' a memorial to Hanna Phillips, of this parish, who died on the eve of wedlock in 1707.

DUNVALL.

Upon leaving the church, a meadow path soon brings us to Dunvall, a remarkable old timbered mansion of the Elizabethan era. Its massive oak beams display great variety of treatment, and are entirely guiltless of ironwork, being joined together by long wooden pegs; while many of them are scored on the surface with curious lines and hatchings, private marks of the craftsmen who fashioned them, perhaps.

The hall with its open staircase, oak panelling and wide, lattice-paned windows, has a delightfully old-world appearance, and probably remains much as originally built.

Dunvall formerly belonged to a branch of the Acton family, in whose days the old house boasted a library of rare and curious volumes, including a 'Breeches' Bible, dated 1582. But the Actons have long since departed, their relics and curios have been dispersed, and the place thereof knoweth them no more.

So now, having done with Dunvall, we take our departure in a south-westerly direction; faring along, up-hill and down-dale, amidst green meadows and golden wheatfields, where the labourers are plying their peaceful, rural toil; while the clack! clack! of the 'reaper-and-binder' sounds merrily through the still air.

Emerging from labyrinthine lanes, we strike the Wenlock road three miles from Bridgnorth, and march on thence into the village of Morville. Calling in at the clerk's cottage for the key of the church—a key of Brobdingnagian size—we push on past the pretty, rustic post-office, and the village smithy; and then, espying the old grey church and Hall away in the vale to our left, we climb over a stile, and make our way thitherwards.

St. Gregory's church at Morville is an interesting edifice of great antiquity, though no part of the earlier structure, which stood here in Edward the Confessor's days, is now in existence. Dating from the early years of the twelfth century, the present church constituted a cell subject to Shrewsbury Abbey; and our cherished and most respectable Leland did not fail to take note of the place, as he journeyed by from Wenlock to Bridgnorth, describing it as 'a little priory, or cell, at Morfeilde, on the right hand as I entered the village.'

Morville church has the long chancel usually seen in collegiate foundations, the semi-headed chancel arch being curiously depressed, and having rudely sculptured capitals, and billet mouldings. Large, very quaintly carved wooden effigies of the four Evangelists, are fixed against the wall just below the corbels of the nave roof; but they are probably not now in their original positions.

The large, cylindrical font is enriched with primitive, arcaded ornamentation; and two very ancient oak muniment chests stand in the adjacent aisle. In the course of repairs, some years ago, traces of colour-decoration, or fresco, were detected under the whitewash on the south wall.

Upon regaining the high-road we pass the Acton Arms, a well-to-do-looking wayside hostelry. Then Morville Hall comes in sight, a grey stone mansion with projecting wings, occupying the site of the ancient priory, whose last Prior, Richard Marshall, died in 1558.

En route to Aston Eyres, the tall trees of Aldenham avenue greet the eye pleasantly, though the Hall itself is hidden. At this diminutive village of Aston we find a church of proportionate scale, the only feature whereof that need detain us being the remarkable sculptured panel shewn in our sketch. It stands above the south door, and, protected by the projecting porch, is still in an excellent state of preservation, though evidently of very great antiquity.

As may be seen, there is much quaint character about the several figures, which are carved in high relief. In the centre we see the Saviour, palm-branch in hand, riding into Jerusalem upon an ass, which is followed by its colt; to the right a seated figure strews branches in the way, while another man is in the act of casting his cloak upon the ground.

It is recorded that Robert Fitz Aer caused this church to be built, between the years 1132 and 1148; and to his piety we are doubtless indebted for this interesting piece of sculpture.

Incorporated with some large farm buildings, on the north side of the churchyard, we find considerable remains of the thirteenth-century manor-house of the Fitz Aers; part of the great hall and the two-storied domestic buildings, with a circular newel stairway, being traceable in the fabric of a big stone barn.

In the quiet country towards Wenlock, on the foothills of the Clees, lie the sleepy hamlets of Monk Hopton and Acton Round; the latter boasting a restored church, with tombs of the Acton family, and some remains of a hall of Queen Anne's time, now turned into a farm-house.

Retracing our steps to Morville, we plunge into a hollow, sequestered lane, and, after passing a rustic mill, and negotiating one or two rather breakneck 'pitches,' we win onwards past Meadowley cover to the brow of a steep, wooded ridge, whose base is washed by the Mor brook.

Presently a little grey church and an old ruddy manor-house are seen, keeping company among the trees that top the hill beyond the narrow vale at our feet; and that is Upton Cressett.

We now bend our steps towards the church, which, rising amidst the fields, a stone's-throw aside from the lane, seems part and parcel of the tranquil landscape. Standing thus alone, enshrouded by trees, under the lee of the sheltering hill, there is something pensive in the attitude of this ancient house of prayer; as though the place were lost in dreams of 'the days that are no more.'

The westering sun, glinting through the trees, spreads the shadows broad athwart the quiet green graveyard. The drowsy hum of insects pervades the autumnal air, the homing rooks make a pleasant sound in the tall elms beside the Hall, and the distant lowing of cattle comes faintly to our ears.

Upton Cressett church is an ancient, stone-built structure, surmounted at its western end by a low, twelfth-century broach spire, a very good and early example of that kind of steeple. The wide timbered porch, seen in our sketch, encloses a fine Norman doorway of three orders, having carved capitals and a semicircular arch ornamented with chevron mouldings.

Of similar but even richer character is the chancel arch, which consists of four distinct orders, with traces of a fifth; a most unusual elaboration for a remote village church such as this.

The thick stone walls are pierced by small Norman and later

30

windows, the east window itself being curiously narrow, a mere lancet light. There was evidently a north aisle at one time, its blocked arches being visible outside the church. The font is of a peculiar shape, like an urn, with slender, rounded arches incised upon it, and rude cable mouldings.

A door in the south wall of the chancel gives access to the Cressett chapel, which has a high-pitched, open-timbered roof, and contains a seventeenth-century oak communion table. Traces of faded frescoes are visible upon the wall; into which is let a small brass, dated 1640, in memory of Richard Cressett, a member of the distinguished family which in bygone times lived in the adjacent Hall.

As 'Ultone,' Upton Cressett figures in Domesday Survey. In 1165, Upton formed part of the Barony of Fitz Alan, being held for some generations by the descendants of Alan de Upton. The Cressetts first appear as Lords of Upton towards the close of the fourteenth century, when, the male line of the Uptons becoming extinct, Thomas Cressett succeeded to Upton, and gave his name to the place. Richard Cressett, builder of the existing house, held the honourable office of Sheriff of Shropshire, as did many of his descendants in after years.

Let us now stroll across to the Hall. As indicated upon a panel let into the wall, the house was erected in the year 1580, and the fine chimney stacks and diapered gables which figure in our sketch date from about that period. Viewed from the north-east, its chequered gables, bronzed, lichen-clad roofs, and wrinkled chimneys, rise with charming effect against the dappled blue of the sky.

Internally the house has been much modernized, but some of the older chambers are nicely wainscoted; and the 'chapel room' upstairs is divided by the great beams of the roof into bays, with arched braces and a sort of embattled cornice, all as massive and simple as possible.

Beyond a green courtyard rises the Gatehouse, a curious little building with ivied gables and quaint angle turrets, apparently coeval with the mansion, and, like it, constructed of fine, timeworn brickwork, of a pleasant mellow hue. The gateway passage shews remnants of antique gothic lettering, now illegible from decay. A stairway in one

THE GATEHOUSE
UPTON CRESSETT
UPTON·CRESSETT·HALL

of the turrets leads to several small chambers, in one of which Prince Rupert is said to have slept. Some fine though damaged plaster-work in this room displays the usual Tudor emblems, and the word · IESV · upon a heart, all delicately executed.

The course of the moat, the ancient well, and the site of the drawbridge can still be identified, a gigantic oak tree marking the outlet of the former. There is said to have been, in the olden times, a subterranean passage running from here to Holgate Castle, in Corve Dale; but, as that is six miles distant as the crow flies, the tradition must be accepted cum grano salis.

Bidding farewell to Upton Cressett, we work a course back to Bridgnorth by a different route. This leads us near to The Hay, a place where, long, long ago, the Lady Juliana de Kenley owned certain lands, which, as is recorded, she disposed of for the moderate rental of one pair of white gloves, value one halfpenny, 'in lieu of all suit of Court and Halimot.'

Once more we pace the now familiar 'petrified kidneys' of the old Severn-side town, and so come at last to our nocturnal lodging place. Turning in for the night, we quickly lose ourselves in the arms of Morpheus, our day's adventures are finally 'rounded with a sleep'—and the rest is silence.

Stocks & Whipping Post
at Stockton.

BETWEEN SEVERN AND CLEE.

THE morning mists hang white and chill about the ghostly landscape, like a world rolled up in cotton wool, as, turning our backs upon Bridgnorth, we hie away southwards adown the vale of Severn. The sun, robbed of his rays, and wan as the moon herself, looks over the low hills of the Staffordshire border; and a fleecy, mackerel sky, gives promise of a likely day in store for folk who fare abroad.

Descending the hill and crossing Severn bridge, we push onward at a good round pace along Hospital Street, so named from the Leper House, or Hospital, which in mediæval days occupied the site of yonder old brick mansion, called St. James's, which now comes in sight among the trees upon our left.

A mile farther on, where the road bifurcates, we are within a measurable distance of the Gallows Leasow, the site of another grim relic of feudal times. Here, too, is Danesford; a name that carries us still farther back into the past.

Towards the close of the ninth century, the Danes, driven out of Essex by King Alfred, sought refuge in this locality, and entrenched themselves in the great Forest of Morf, which in those days covered all this countryside.

Presently as we travel along, Quatford church-tower is seen overlooking a bend of the river. Quatford, the Cwth-Briege of the Saxon Chronicle, is a very ancient place, the earliest records of which take us back to King Alfred's days.

In the year 896 the Danes, to quote an old chronicler, 'toke their way towards Wales, and came to Quadruge, nere to the River of Severne, where, upon the borders thereof, they buildid them a Castle.' Here, on the spot overlooking the Severn still called the Danish Camp, they spent the winter, 'not without dislike of their lodging, and cold entertainment'; withdrawing eventually into East Anglia again.

Towards the close of the eleventh century, Roger de Belesme began the building of his 'New House and Borough,' mentioned in Domesday, which probably occupied the site of the earlier Danish encampment. After the death of Earl Roger, his son, Robert de Belesme, removed both castle and Burgh to the spot where Bridgnorth now stands. 'At Quatford,' says John Leland, 'yett appeare great Tokens of a Pyle, or Mannour Place, longing that tyme to Robert de Belesmo.'

Occupying the summit of a rocky standstone knoll, Quatford church is approached by a long flight of steps, leading up to the south porch. In accordance with a romantic vow, the church was dedicated to St. Mary Magdalene, as a memorial of and thank-offering for escape from shipwreck, by Adeliza, wife of Earl Roger the Norman; and was consecrated in the year 1086. The chancel arch and adjacent walls, built of a peculiar porous stone called tufa, or travertin, quite different from the rest of the structure, may possibly have formed part of that ancient edifice.

In a meadow near Hillhouse Farm, a quarter of a mile north-east of Quatford church, we come to the 'Forest Oak,' a queer old stunted tree which might be of almost any age, with its two short, gnarled stems, supporting a head of wrinkled foliage. So let us give this venerable weed the benefit of the doubt, by accepting the local tradition that here, beneath its shade, the Countess Adeliza met Earl Roger her husband after her perilous voyage, and prevailed upon him to erect the votive church to St. Mary Magdalene, at Quatford.

Away across the Severn, at Eardington, is (or was) a small farm called The Moors; a place that gives rise to a quaint ceremony, performed every year in London. On October 22, a proclamation is made in the Exchequer as follows: 'Oyez! Oyez! Oyez! Tenants and occupiers of a piece of waste ground called "The Moors," in the County of Salop, come forth and do your service!' The tenants in question then proceed to do sergeantry by cutting two faggots of wood, one with a hatchet, the other with a bill-hook.

The fons et origo of this curious feudal custom has long since been lost in the mists of antiquity; but the earliest recorded instance of the service was in the reign of King John, 1210.

Bidding adieu to Quatford, we descend the hill, pass the 'Danery,' or Deanery, Inn, and the site of Quatford bridge, and plod on between hedgerows bejewelled with glistening dewdrops. The 'charm' of the birds, to use the Shropshire phrase, no longer enlivens the byway; but a solitary songster every now and again wakes the echoes of woodland or coppice. Atalanta, yonder, taking heart of grace, suns her glossy wings on a spray of the 'swete bramble floure'; while the rabbits, startled at our approach, bob off to their burrows in the sandy bank.

Dudmaston Hall is left away to our right, and anon we come to Quat, a mite of a place whose name, derived from Coed, a wood, shews it once stood within the bounds of Morf Forest.

Some three miles to the eastward, close to the Staffordshire border, stands Gatacre Hall, the ancestral home of the family of that ilk, which has been settled here, it is said, ever since the reign of Edward the Confessor. Major-General Sir W. Gatacre, one of the victors of Omdurman, is a distinguished scion of this good old stock, having first seen the light, if we are rightly informed, at Gatacre Hall.

The existing mansion, a modern, red-brick edifice, seated in a beautiful locality, has usurped the place of the original house, which must have been unique of its kind, to judge from the following description.

'It was built,' writes Camden, 'of a dark grey free stone, coated with a thin greenish vitrified substance, about the thickness of a crown piece. The hall was nearly an exact square, and most remarkably constructed. At each corner, in the middle of each side, and in the centre, was an immense oak tree, hewed nearly square, and without branches; set with their heads on large stones laid about a foot deep in the ground, and with their roots uppermost, which roots, with a few rafters, formed a compleat arched roof. The floor was of oak boards three inches thick, not sawed, but plainly chipped.'

Beyond Hampton Load ferry we ascend a lane shewing evidences of having been paved. Coming to a corner where four ways meet, we see, by the laneside, the old stone Cross illustrated here; a monolith about 5 feet in height, upon a circular stone base. On each side of the rounded head a cross is faintly distinguishable; but, as a passer-by truly remarks, 'They've yacked un and yowed un, so as you canna very well make out what it be all about.'

THE BUTTER CROSS, ALVELEY.

When and why the cross was erected there is no record to shew, but it is evidently of great antiquity, and probably was used as a meeting place for holding a sort of open-air market. It is sometimes called the Butter Cross, the lower stone being supposed to represent a cheese, and the round head a pat of butter!

A quarter of an hour's walk brings us to Alveley, a rather untidy village, scattered higgledy-piggledy along a crooked roadway. St. Mary's church, however, proves interesting enough to make amends for other shortcomings.

Many styles of architecture, from Norman to late Decorated, are represented here. The Norman nave has clerestory windows, in one of which we espy some good pre-Reformation glass; and a flattish oak roof spans the whole.

At the east end of the south aisle rises a beautiful fifteenth-century chantry chapel, dedicated to St. Mary, upon the walls whereof considerable remains of ancient frescoes are still discernible. They appear to represent, the Fall: the Redemption of Man: the Annunciation:

and the Salutation; but, as they are all much worn and faded, this is somewhat conjectural.

Upon the wall of the adjacent aisle is a curious old altar-frontal, which formerly belonged to St. Mary's chantry. It dates from about 1470, and is wrought upon coloured silk, depicting the Church at rest in Abraham's bosom. The figure of Abraham is admirably portrayed, his countenance being of a decidedly Jewish cast; while the Church, in the form of a group of diminutive figures, is seen snugly ensconced in a sort of napkin, held between Abraham's outstretched hands.

The west tower is early Norman, and, in spite of later excrescences, is probably the oldest part of the church. Nor must we omit to mention the very ancient 'excommunication' door, now blocked, near the west end ot the north aisle. An inscription of some interest to the Freemason fraternity appears upon the outer lintel of this doorway; to wit: ANO · DOMINI · 1585 : IHON · DAΛIS · FREEMASON : This fine church was well restored by Blomfield, in 1878.

From Alveley we make a détour to visit Pool Hall, which is

interesting mainly from its past associations, the present house being a somewhat shabby, neglected-looking building of no great antiquity. 'Polehous' first figures in history about the middle of the fourteenth century, when we find it in the possession of Henry de la Pole. The Manor of Alveley, in which Pool Hall is situated, formed one of the four manors held by Algar, Earl of Mercia, before the Normans had penetrated into this part of England.

Retracing our steps to Alveley, we drop down to the ferry at Potter's Load, a pleasant, sequestered spot, where the ferryman's picturesque cottage is the only habitation in sight. A shady path, climbing steeply up through the woods, soon brings us to Highley village. The place, as its name suggests, stands at a considerable elevation, affording frequent glimpses of the surrounding country, a hilly-and-daley region.

Conspicuous at the top of the village rises its parish church, on the south side whereof we find the interesting fragment of a Calvary cross depicted in the sketch on p. 213. The broken shaft, which has angle chamfers terminating in small heads, stands upon a massive base edged with bold cable mouldings, and ornamented with sphinx-like faces at the corners. On the west side of the base is the curious crocketed niche seen in the cut; it may conjecturally have been used to display the Paschal light at Easter-tide. The southern side has a hand and the letters I·H·C cut upon it.

The adjacent church, though ancient, is somewhat featureless; and the Church-house, an antiquated structure of timber and plaster overlooking the graveyard, seems quite the oldest residence in the village.

Southward from Highley, the Severn itself forms for several miles the Shropshire boundary, an outlying elbow of Staffordshire coming in upon the east, and giving a curious local twist to the frontier hereabouts.

Until comparatively recent times, there was an isolated cantle of Shropshire lying derelict, so to speak, far away towards the east, upon the confines of Worcester and Stafford. The quiet old townlet of Halesowen, with its ruined Premonstratensian Abbey founded by

King John, was formerly included in Shropshire; as was also the curious little chapel of St. Kenelm, on the slopes of the Clent Hills, and the pleasant estate of the Leasowes, with its groves and pseudo-classic ruined temples, in the taste of the last century, and its memories of Shenstone the poet.

But we digress, so now, revenons à nos moutons.

Laying a southwesterly course from Highley, we set out anon for Kinlet Hall, a place seated in a wild, secluded locality, on the borders of Wyre Forest. Our way lies in the main through a country of low,

KINLET HALL.

tumbled hills, thatched with woodland; one or two colliery chimneys, emitting grimy smoke, seeming out of place amid these green, pastoral landscapes.

After passing the vicarage we enter Kinlet Park, a tract of undulating country about 500 acres in area, containing bosky dells and sylvan glades, where flourish some of the finest oaks and beeches in the county.

The Hall and church soon come in sight, the former a fine, spacious structure of brick, with stone quoins, built in the year 1729 by an ancestor of the present proprietor; the original half-timbered mansion, which stood nearer the church, having been pulled down at that time.

Though lacking the picturesque variety of an earlier style, Kinlet Hall impresses one by a certain serene dignity as it rises, four-square and ruddy, and flanked by large arched gateways, from the smooth, close-cropped greensward of the home-park; a worthy example of an English country residence of the early Georgian period. Some good ancestral portraits lend interest to the interior, including likenesses of the builder of the existing mansion, and his lady.

At the time of the Norman Conquest, the estate of Kinlet appertained to Editha, Edward the Confessor's widow, and in after years passed successively to the houses of Cornewall and of Blount. The Blounts, as Camden tells us, were 'an antient, illustrious, and numerous family in these parts, who have extended their branches a great way, and who certainly have their name from their yellow hair.' Kinlet eventually came into the possession of the Baldwyns, a widely connected Shropshire family, and is now the residence of Captain C. Baldwyn-Childe.

Kinlet church, nestling in a grove of trees almost under the shadow of the Hall, is a small but interesting cruciform structure. In the Blount chapel we find monuments to various members of that family, as well as to the Childes. The finest of these is a richly canopied table-tomb, with the figures of Sir George Blount and his wife kneeling beneath niches, a recumbent effigy in the arched vault below, and a quaint Latin epitaph alongside. This knight was a distinguished soldier, and sometime High Sheriff of Salop; he died in the year 1581. Against the adjacent wall there is a curious representation of the Crucifixion, in stone, and there are one or two sixteenth-century marble monuments in the chancel.

Some idea of the exterior of Kinlet church may be gathered from the little sketch on the previous page, which shews the half-timbered clerestory, the pretty gable-end of the Blount chapel, and a certain small stone structure which rises in the churchyard. It is square on plan, with an arched recess on each side, the one towards the west having a shallow niche on the inner face. It appears to have been surmounted by a cross, of which the base-stone may be seen upon the apex of the roof.

Dotted here and there about the valley of the Rea, as it comes down from Brown Clee Hill, are a number of obscure villages and isolated hamlets, which have remained as primitive, probably, as any in all broad Shropshire. It is the country, par excellence, of stiff red clay, as the oft-repeated name of 'Clee' plainly indicates; and its sunny barley fields, its orchards and bosky woodlands, have given rise to the local adage:

'Blest is the eye 'twixt Severn and Wye,
But thrice blessed he 'twixt Severn and Clee!'

Ditton Priors, with its interesting old church, carved oak rood-screen, stalls and lectern, lies under the shadow of Brown Clee, near the head-waters of the Rea. Cleobury North, on the Ludlow road, had a church subject to Brecon Priory as long ago as Henry the First's time. One or two epitaphs in the graveyard here are worth a passing notice.

Then we come to Burwarton, whose inn, the Boyne Arms, offers bed and board for the wayfarer in a better style than one is wont to find in this remote locality, where as a rule the traveller is fortunate who, like the proverbial Scotsman, is 'contented wi' little, an' cantie wi' mair.'

Burwarton church is mainly of Norman date, having a plain, semi-headed chancel arch of that period, and a little carved woodwork.

Brown Clee Hill, lying due west, may be easily climbed from here; and the view from the top, described on a previous page, will well repay the scramble.

A mile south-east is Aston Botterel, where, in the south aisle of the church, may be seen an altar-tomb with pillared canopy to one of the Botterels, who held the Manor of Aston of the Earls of Arundel. At the Bold, hard by, are some slight remains of an ancient building, probably a chapel.

Proceeding on our way adown the vale, we come presently to Wheathill, a place that in the Conqueror's time formed a portion of the vast estates of Earl Roger de Montgomery. Wheathill church is of Norman origin, having a fine south doorway with cable moulding, and tympanum with axe-hewn ornamentation. The Hakets were the great folks here in olden times, John Haket, Rector of 'Wheathull,' being mysteriously drowned in the Teme, near Ludlow, in 1342.

Some forty minutes later we find ourselves at Stottesdon; our way thither leading by unfrequented lanes across the Rea brook. Here we happen upon a church which, though restored about thirty years ago, retains many points of interest to the antiquary.

Stottesdon church has one of the finest Norman fonts in the county. It is ornamented with an interlaced border, and other enrichments; and the carvings of the west doorway are so rude and primitive, they might have formed part of the earlier church known to have existed here in Saxon times. The base of the tower is also possibly pre-Norman, while the Wrickton chantry dates from the fourteenth century.

In 1085, Roger de Montgomery gave Stottesdon church, with all its rich endowments, to his great Abbey at Shrewsbury. When visiting Stottesdon in the year 1290, so poor was this neighbourhood, that Bishop Swinfield had to send all the way to Kidderminster market for provender, and for shoes for his coach horses.

Bestowed by the Conqueror upon Roger de Montgomery, the 'Marquis de Carabas' of the Welsh border, Stottesdon manor became the caput, or chief place, of one of the Shropshire Hundreds. Becoming forfeit to the Crown, the King bestowed the manor, about 1159, on Godfrey de Gamages, in which family it remained until the year 1230. Thereafter we find de Plaesto and de Seagrave enrolled as over-lords of Stottesdon; claiming free-warren, and holding free-courts, with all the rights and privileges thereto attached.

Pushing on towards Cleobury Mortimer through a rough, broken country, we come by-and-by to a farmhouse called Walltown, occupying the site of a Roman encampment, whose outer lines are still clearly traceable. In Blakeway's time, the old road from Cleobury to Bridgnorth passed directly through the centre of the camp, 'entering at the Prætorian, and passing out at the Decuman Gate,' but its course has since been altered.

Leaving Neen Savage in the vale upon our right, we cut off a corner by a lane that drops steeply to the Rea; and after sighting the broken walls of Lloyd's Paper-mill, looking like a ruined castle, we make our entry into Cleobury Mortimer, with the tall, twisted spire of St. Mary's church rising above the housetops, like a crooked, beckoning finger.

So, while beating up for the 'Talbot,' let us call to mind a few facts about the history of the town. 'The village of Clebyri,' to quote Leland once again, 'standythe in the Rootes by est of Cle Hills, seven myles from Ludlow, in the Way to Beaudeley.' At the time of Domesday Survey 'Claiberie' was held by Queen Editha, and in mediæval days formed, with the circumjacent country, part of the great Honour of Mortimer. These haughty Mortimers, indeed, ruled the roost for many a long day at Cleobury; but their castle was destroyed during the Barons' Wars, and the site alone, 'nighe the churche by Northe,' was to be seen in Leland's time.

Robert Dudley, Earl of Leicester, Queen Elizabeth's 'sweet Robin,' was for a while the lord of Cleobury. In the 'Lives of the Dudleys' we read: 'He was a compleat Gentleman in all suitable employments; an exact seaman, an excellent architect, mathematician, physician, chymist and what not. He was a handsome, personable man, tall of stature, red haired, and of an admirable comport; and above all noted

CLEOBURY-
MORTIMER,
FROM "THE WELLS.

for riding the great horse for tilting, and for his being the first of all that taught a dog to sit in order to catch partridges.'

At Cleobury was born in the fourteenth century William Langland, the 'Poet of the Lollards.' About the year 1362, Langland composed those 'Visions of Piers Plowman,' which have caused their author to be acknowledged as one of the earliest of England's songsters.

So much, then, for the brave days of old. Cleobury Mortimer as we see it to-day is a long, straggling, torpid townlet, whose agricultural proclivities are chequered by the mining industries carried on around Titterstone Clee Hill, and the woodcraft of the people who dwell in the neighbouring Forest of Wyre.

Having secured a night's billet at the Talbot Inn, we sally forth again and proceed to spy out the land. Out in the High Street is seen a block of timeworn sandstone, whereon, according to a credible tradition, young Arthur Tudor's body was laid, he having died while travelling this way from Ludlow Castle to Bewdley.

A few yards farther on we come to the parish church, a noble old pile dedicated to St. Mary the Virgin, the central and dominant feature of Cleobury town. Its graceful arches and elegant fenestration mark the Early English period; though the tower, the oldest portion of the fabric, dates back to Norman times. Far aloft soars the tall wooden steeple, whose old warped timbers, stripped of their clumsy boarding, are now being clad in a weatherproof garb of stout oak shingles.

A large, handsome south porch gives access to the interior, where, inter alia, we observe a remarkably shapely chancel arch, and some modern stained glass in the east window, a memorial to William Langland, the poet, who may be descried therein, dreaming over his 'visions' as he reclines on a bank, with Malvern Hills away in the background.

A further ramble about the town introduces us to Cleobury College, a handsome building in a pleasant situation, erected, as a tablet informs us, by Sir Lacon W. Childe, of Kinlet, in 1740, and recently enlarged and improved. Then, down in a hollow of the highway, we stumble across the quaint view which our artist has here reproduced; the crooked church steeple soaring heavenwards above a tall Scotch fir, while the foreground is occupied by an arched grotto enclosing the crystal-clear, perennial spring, called the Wells, whence the townsfolk draw their unfailing supply of water.

From Cleobury Mortimer we will make an excursion towards Bewdley; our route, for a large part of the way, lying through the heart of Wyre Forest. The forest is worth a visit, though nowadays the 'tall oaks' of Camden's time are conspicuous by their absence, having long since been cut down and carried off to smelt the iron ore of the Midlands, ere 'sea-coal' came into use.

> 'When soon the goodlie Wyre, that wonted was soe hie,
> Her statelie top to reare, ashamed to behold
> Her straighte and goodlie Woods unto the furnace sold;
> And looking on herself, by her decay doth see
> The miserie wherein her sister forests bee.'

Covering a broken, dimpled country, with many quiet sylvan nooks enlivened by streams and brooklets, Wyre Forest is still a pleasant, wild, out-of-the-way district to ramble in; and is a favourite haunt of birds, butterflies, beetles, moths, and similar 'small deer,' as many a naturalist knows. The former extent and importance of the forest may be gathered from the fact that the County of Worcester is named after it, and that to this day it remains one of the largest tracts of woodland in the Marches of Wales. Old, disused coalpits here and there, shew that the coveted 'black diamonds' lie underfoot, though of a quality so poor as scarce to repay the cost of winning—'thank goodness,' one is minded to say.

So by cross-country cuts and woodland ways we ramble through the forest, until, just short of the Bewdley road, we get a pretty peep of Dowles Manor-house, an ancient timbered dwelling seated in a dell, embosomed amidst trees, and bearing the date 1560 cut upon one of its old black beams. Then we come to Dowles church, a fifteenth-century building, though it doesn't look it, having been encased in brick about a hundred years ago.

Strolling along the towing-path by Severn side, we presently catch sight of

> 'Fair seated Bewdley, a delightful Towne,
> Which Wyre's tall oaks with shady branches crown.'

Situated on the western bank of the Severn, 'the Towne of Beaudley is sett on the Syde of an Hill, so comely, a Man cannot wish to see a Towne better,' as friend Leland remarks. 'At the Rising of the Sunne from East,' he tells us, 'the whole Towne glittereth as it were of gould'; an observation which shews that the famous antiquary had an eye for the picturesque.

DOWLES MANOR HOUSE.

Bewdley Bridge, an elegant stone structure, built by Telford about a century ago in place of an older one, connects Bewdley itself with its staid old neighbour Wribbenhall. 'To this bridge resort many flatt long Vessells, to carry up and downe all manner of Marchandize,' writes Leland; but the railways have driven the traffic from the river, so that nowadays the merchants' stores and warehouses stand empty and idle beside the silent highway.

Time was when this ancient borough of Bewdley drove a thriving trade in Welsh flannels, and other produce of the border; shipping her wares down-stream to Bristol, or sending them away on pack-horses by bridle-paths, such as the hollow way called the Welsh Gate that runs below Ticknell hill. The old 'George' posting-house, with a handful of substantial-looking houses, mostly of the Georgian era, lend a respectable, well-to-do air to the town; but its parish church, at the top of the main street, is unspeakably ugly; a red-brick abomination of the true 'churchwarden' type.

Bewdley has been a borough town ever since the days of Edward IV.; and, until 1885, returned its own member to Parliament. A quarter of a mile south of the town stands the old manor-house of Ticknell.

'Bewdele, the Sanctuary Towne, hath hard by it the Kynge's Maner of Tikile, standing on a Hill.' At Ticknell was formerly held the famous Court of the Marches; and hither, in 1502, the body of Prince Arthur was brought, after his death while travelling from Ludlow. The earlier house, mentioned by Leland, was destroyed by the Covenanters, but the mansion now standing has some pretensions to antiquity.

The Tenbury and Bewdley railway, as it traverses the valley of Dowles brook, gives us some interesting glimpses of the Forest, whose russet foliage glows resplendent in the level rays of this September sunshine. After passing Cleobury station we run between steep, rocky banks, fringed with broom, heather and bracken, getting every now and again wide views of forest land overtopped by distant hills. Then Mawley Hall is seen, an old-time abode of the Blounts; and, running past a large seventeenth-century brick-and-stone house called Reaside farm, we come by-and-by to Neen Sollers, a quiet agricultural village with an ancient cruciform church, whose old grey tower and spire are seen overtopping the nearer trees. Thenceforward we travel on amidst tranquil, rural landscapes, where the ruddy apples lie in piles about the orchards, and the willow-fringed Teme winds along through the vale on her way to meet Father Severn.

Arrived at Tenbury station we quit the train, and, passing near the Castle Tump, a grass-grown mound marking the approach to the ancient ford, we traverse an old stone bridge and trudge on into

Tenbury, a pleasant little Worcestershire town on the banks of Teme, a famous fishing river. The Swan Hotel at the entrance to the town looks the picture of an angler's inn; so there we will rest awhile.

A meadow path by Temeside leads us towards Burford, of whose fine church we presently obtain an effective view, its broad, richly embattled tower grouping prettily, as shewn in our sketch, with a quaint churchyard cross, and the feathery foliage of the surrounding trees.

Burford church is of very ancient foundation, but has been much altered at various times, and has recently undergone a thorough restoration by Mr. Aston Webb, the well-known architect. There is much to interest the ecclesiologist in this handsome, well-cared-for church; but chief among its attractions is the wealth and variety of its monuments.

A low table-tomb in the centre of the chancel bears the figure of Edmund Cornwaylle, clad in plate armour, and wearing the gilded spurs of an equitis aurati. Beneath a handsome ogee canopy in the adjacent wall lies the effigy of a female, with the following inscription: HERE LYETH THE BODY OF THE MOST NOBLE ELIZABETH, DAUGHTER OF JOHN OF GAUNT DUKE OF LANCASTER, OWN SISTER TO KING HENRY IV., WIFE OF JOHN HOLLAND, EARL OF HUNTINGTON, AND DUKE OF EXETER; AFTER MARRIED TO SIR JOHN CORNWALL, KNIGHT OF THE GARTER. SHE DIED THE 4TH YEAR OF HENRY VI. AÑ DÑI MCCCCXXVI.

A curious brass in the north-east corner of the chancel, bearing an inscription in old Norman-French, commemorates Dame Elizabeth, wife of Sir Elmon de Cornewaylle, a fourteenth-century knight. On the wall above is a remarkable triptych, a memento of the Cornewall family, said to be the work of one Melchior Salaboss, a foreign artist.

There is a fine fifteenth-century font; and in the south chancel wall we notice two curious little 'heart-shrines,' small circular receptacles with lids, beneath a pointed arch. The custom was in early times, when a nobleman died abroad, to embalm his heart, and send it home to be buried amongst his kinsfolk; under the circumstances a convenient method of sepulture.

After the Mortimers, the Cornewalls ruled here for generations as Barons of Burford, being under service to find five men to fight in Edward the Third's Welsh wars. The Ledwyche Brook, flowing into the Teme near Burford church, gives its name to Ledwyche farm, in bygone times the home of the famous Benbows.

Retracing our steps to Tenbury station, a two-mile walk brings us to Boraston, scenes of rural industry enlivening the way. In yonder upland field the harvesters are busy carting the wheat, the golden shocks shewing up sharp and clear against the purple background of the Clee Hills; while the wavering hum of a threshing-machine drones a homely accompaniment. Then we descend into a vale, and trudge along the green alleys of a hop-yard, the fragrant bines drooping beneath their wealth of fruit and foliage, and clinging each to its neighbour with slender, outstretched tendrils.

Boraston comprises a handful of rustic dwellings, scattered about a little church, one or two of the older ones displaying half-timbered gables towards the road. Boraston church has been much restored, but retains several early cusped windows, and an old roof whose rafters are carried half-way down the southward wall. On either side the nave is a curious, plain, arched recess, the use whereof is not apparent; and there are traces of a very ancient doorway, now built up. The apsidal east end, a south porch, and a shingled bell-turret above the western gable, are the most salient points of the exterior.

Nash chapel, a mile or so to the north, is almost a replica of Boraston. This church has been quaintly described by Mr. Cranage as, 'a "Decorated" building which is *not decorated*.' Court-of-Hill is the most interesting house in this locality.

In the broken country west of Boraston lies the hamlet of Greete, with a small, aisle-less church, dedicated to St. James, of Norman and Early English date. The pleasant rural vicarage and oldfashioned Court-house farm are almost its only neighbours, but about a mile to the west stands Stoke House, a plain but good example of a brick-built Tudor residence.

Very rustic and unsophisticated are the country folk hereabouts, even in these fin-de-siècle days; and it is within living memory that Parson J——, coming to take up his new duty in a neighbouring parish, walked into the village driving his cow before him! Time was when some of these country parsons were mighty hunters before the Lord. There is a story of one of them who, when about to start for the meet, got wind that his Bishop was coming to pay him a visitation. Jumping into bed, scarlet jacket and all, he leaves word with his old housekeeper that he is ill upstairs, and the tale is repeated to his lordship. 'Dear me, I'm very sorry; tell him I'll walk up and see how he's getting on,' says the Bishop. The message is duly delivered, whereupon our Nimrod sends back his reply, 'No, no, it's quite impossible; I'm down with a shocking bad attack of *scarlet* fever!'

The road ascends as we make our way northwards, with quarries and lime-works defacing the heights that buttress Clee Hill on this side. After a stiffish bit of collar work we come to Whitton Chapel, a simple, solitary building, with a good though plain Norman south doorway, and a primitive-looking old tower.

A bowshot farther on we enter the demesne of Whitton Court, a charming, seventeenth-century mansion, whose ruddy old brick gables, clustered chimney stacks and mullioned windows, all wreathed in luxuriant ivy and set against a background of autumnal foliage, make as pleasant a picture as one could wish to see. Inside and out alike, this venerable abode is a delight to the lover of things antique and curious, its owners having displayed rare good taste in such renovations as have been found needful. Though in the main of Elizabethan style, the oldest portions of the house date back as early as the fourteenth century; and some richly carved woodwork, some good pictures and curious old tapestry, are features of the interior. An admirable sketch of Whitton Court appeared in Mr. Oliver Baker's 'Ludlow Town and Neighbourhood.'

Tinker's Hill is full in view towards the west as we push on for Hope Bagot, its tree-begirt slopes crowned by the old British earthwork called Caynham Camp, of which the Parliamentarians availed themselves when besieging the town of Ludlow. In the vale below lies Caynham church, an ancient but much restored edifice, which has a curious triple chancel arch of rather unusual character.

Ashford Bowdler, with its quaint old church overlooking the Teme, lies but a few miles beyond, in a picturesque nook of the county adjacent to the Herefordshire border.

Hope Bagot itself stands high up in the world, looking out across the pleasant vale of Teme from its 'hope,' or upland valley, among the foothills of Titterstone Clee. So now we stroll on to the church, which is seen a short distance away under the shoulder of Knowl Hill.

It is an ancient place, and, with its grey stone walls and timbered porch, falls in pleasingly with its rustic environment, tempting the wayfarer to make a closer acquaintance. Many notable objects here meet our gaze, a curious sedilia and piscina in the chancel, to reach which we pass beneath a chancel arch evidently built by the Normans; and the plain, bowl-shaped font is perhaps of equal antiquity, while the carving upon the old oak pulpit calls for a passing notice.

A great dark yew-tree flings its shadow athwart the graveyard, and yonder is the Holy Well, famed in bygone times as a sovereign remedy for curing sore eyes.

But the day wears towards a close, and it behoves us to be up and away; for it is a far cry yet to our night's bivouac at Cleobury Mortimer.

So climbing the steep flank of Titterstone, we win our way to the high road, 'high' indeed at this point, where we stand some 1,250 feet above the sea. Far and wide extends the bounteous landscape, a maze of hill and dale, tilth and pasturage; its remoter features veiled in the soft, warm haze of an autumn afternoon, lending an added charm to every-day, familiar objects.

Swinging along downhill we pass Hopton Wafers, a high-lying village, bowered in trees, beside a rill coming down from Clee. Anon the jolly moon rolls up above the dusky breadths of Wyre Forest; children, homeward-bound from blackberry gathering, give us a 'Good-evening' as they pass; the night wind rustles the silvery willows beside the brook, and a wandering owl raises his melancholy shout from somewhere in the vicinity.

And so beneath the frosty stars we enter old Cleobury again, and, passing the substantial looking manor-house, come to a late meal at the Talbot, just as the curfew bell in the steeple hard by tolls the 'knell of parting day.'

WESTWARD HO! TOWARDS THE WELSH BORDER.

KIRTING the south-eastern suburbs of the County-town, the Minsterley branch line carries us in a devious course beside the Meole Brook, amidst quiet, rural scenery, calling for no particular notice. It is worth while, however, to alight at Hanwood station, in order to take a look at one or two ancient farmhouses that lie not far away.

The finest of these is Moat Hall, a place which, though altered by recent restorations, retains some interesting features. No less than three very handsome old carved oak chimney-pieces are still to be seen, the arms of the Beringtons being traceable among their ornamentation; and the domestic chapel, used in bygone times by those of the 'old faith,' retains its panelled dadoes and rich plaster ceiling. The place was of course haunted; but the ghost, with a fine sense of propriety, none too common amongst such gentry, has departed with a former owner of the estate.

At Hanwood we traverse a small local Black Country, where an outlier of the Shropshire coalfield lies under foot, and where stumpy colliery chimneys and whimsey-wheels deface the nearer landscape. But all this soon gives place to the good open country, as the train approaches Pontesbury station; and tall, cloud-capped hills begin to assert themselves, in the direction whither we are bound.

There is not much to detain the traveller here, for 'Ponsbyri,' as John Leland has it, 'is but an uplandisch Tounlet, 4 miles from Shrewsbyri.' The church, nevertheless, was originally a collegiate

MOAT HALL
HANWOOD.
H. T. T.

foundation, and still boasts a fine, massive tower, besides one or two other good features. Of the 'great Manor Place, or Castelle,' whose ruins Leland saw 'on the south side of the Chirche Yarde,' not one stone now remains upon another. To Pontesbury, some six centuries ago, came the famous Bishop Swinfield; paying, as is recorded, the modest sum of one penny for the ten-mile journey across the hills from Stretton, which may stand, we take it, as a record fare even to this day.

Be that as it may, we now pass on to Minsterley, the terminus of the line; a place that, whatever attractions it may possess, can certainly lay small claim to beauty. Even the Miners' Arms Inn, by its bleak-looking, brick façade, belies the comfort to be found within; and it is not until we come to the parish church that things take a turn for the better.

The little edifice is, perhaps, rather curious than beautiful. Built in the seventeenth century, it has superseded an earlier church of great but unknown antiquity, reputed to have been one of the most ancient ecclesiastical foundations in Shropshire.

Externally, the red-brick front presents a queer combination of skulls, hour-glasses, scythes and cherubs' heads, wrought amidst the classic entablature of the Jacobean portal; a good example of the bad style then in vogue. There is not much else to detain us here, so let us look within.

The interior of Minsterley church is sober, plain and simple; but is relieved from the commonplace by the rich, dark woodwork of its massive oak pulpit and chancel screen, and the great sounding-board which impends above the former.

Suspended from wooden pegs, near the western end of the church, hang some half-dozen Maiden Garlands, or Love Tokens, as they are sometimes called. These curious objects are constructed of ribbons, bows and rosettes, stretched upon a small bee-hive shaped framework. A Love Token was intended to commemorate a betrothed lover who had remained faithful during life, his or her fiancée having died during the time of betrothal. There is, however, another version anent the use of these Maiden Garlands. When a young damsel died, a girl of the same age as the deceased walked at the head of the funeral procession, carrying a Maiden Garland, with a pair of white gloves attached, as an emblem of the purity of the departed. These Garlands at Minsterley bear various dates in the last century, and are among the best preserved of their kind.

Quitting the village by the Bishop's Castle road, we espy upon our right hand the half-timbered gables of Minsterley Hall, a modernized manor-house of the Thynne family, now the property of the Marquess of Bath.

The hills close in as we advance, the road climbing their slopes by a long, steady ascent. Away to the left rise some great refuse-heaps, where lead has been mined at least as far back as the time of the Roman Emperors; for in Shrewsbury Museum may be seen a large 'pig' of lead, found in this neighbourhood, which bears the inscription IMP . HADRANI · AUG.

Pursuing the course of a wimpling brook, our road now leads through the recesses of Hope Vale, a narrow dingle whose sides present an unbroken expanse of greenwood, its verdure looking fresh and bright after the passage of the recent rains, while the carol of many a feathered friend enlivens our onward march. By-and-by this gives place to more open scenery as we approach the Gravel Mine, which is believed to be of Roman origin.

Half a mile away behind the hills lies Shelve, a village given over to mining; whence, by cross-country tracks, the Stiperstones may be ascended. This remarkable range forms one of a series of roughly parallel ridges, which traverse this portion of Shropshire in a north-east to south-westerly direction. Huge, timeworn masses of quartz rock, cropping out here and there upon the skyline, give to these hills a strange, wild appearance; while such names as Devil's Chair, Nipstone Rock, and the like, indicate their traditional origin. One story tells how the Devil, rising up from his chair on the Stiperstones, and taking a three-mile stride across Hope Vale, planted his foot upon the Lord's Stone, a conspicuous rock on the hills to the westward, where, it is said, his footprint may to this day be seen.

Excelsior! is still the order of the day, on resuming our onward route, and the landscape assumes a bleaker look as the road slants steadily upwards. Marsh Pool, a small mere half choked by weeds, appears close at hand below the fernclad slopes of Stapeley Hill; while Corndon soars aloft like a real mountain before us, dwarfing all his lesser neighbours. At the crossways we bear away westwards, striking presently into a rough, rambling cart-track, that leads up the unenclosed hillside.

MITCHELL'S FOLD.

Half a mile of this sort of thing brings us to Mitchell's Fold, which, to compare small things with great, may be called the Stonehenge of Shropshire. A dozen or more large slabs of stone are grouped into an irregular circle, most of the stones having long since fallen down, though three or four of them still remain upright, the tallest standing about 6 feet above the ground.

Tradition, the garrulous jade, has her own story to tell of how Mitchell's Fold first came into existence. Once upon a time, it seems, there was a great famine throughout all this countryside, so that the good folk had much ado to 'keep the wolf from the door.' All they had to live upon was the milk from a white fairy Cow, that, night and morning, came to this spot to be milked. Thus everybody found plenty of milk, provided no one drew more than a pailful.

At length, however, came a wicked old witch, named Mitchell, who proceeded to milk the good white cow into a riddle, or sieve, which she carried in her hand, so that presently the cow ran dry. Discovering the trick that had been played upon her, the cow became highly indignant, and, kicking over the riddle, vanished from the scene, and was never met with in these parts again. Indeed, it is said she turned crazy, and going off into a far country, became transformed into the famous Dun Cow slain by Guy, Earl of Warwick. As for the wicked old witch, she was turned into one of these stones on the hill, and the other stones were set around to keep her safely in; and so it comes to pass that the place to this day bears the name of Mitchell's Fold.

With regard to the beneficent fairy Cow, one is minded to conjecture in what relation she stood to the wonderful Bull, whose exploits we heard of when at Hyssington. That point, however, we respectfully leave for antiquaries to decide, and now push on again for Chirbury.

The west wind greets us lustily, as we tramp in the teeth of the breeze across acres of heather and bracken; pausing now and then to scan the wild moorland prospect, or to watch the gyrations of a brace of plovers, as they circle overhead.

Calling in for a draught of milk at the first farmhouse on the edge of cultivation, we pass the time of day with the master, who gives us a hearty Shropshire greeting. 'You be come to a desprit lonesome place,' remarks our friend; 'and 'tis tedious work traipsin' about them beggarly lands such weather as this; but step in and sit ye down, and my missus 'ool bring us summat to drink.'

So down we sit in the roomy kitchen-place, surrounded by all the homely gear of the goodwife's daily use; taking occasional pulls at Nature's wholesome tipple from big blue china mugs, and discussing the affairs of the countryside like men to the manner born.

Once more afoot, we traverse a stretch of broken, intricate country, and, surmounting a ridge of low hills, drop downwards into the lower reaches of Marrington Dingle, a narrow, picturesque defile watered by the Camlad, whose 'crankling nookes' we hope to explore later on.

On the farther bank of the brook rises Heightley Hall, a mere farmhouse now, though in bygone days it was the ancestral home of the Newtons, an ancient family of more than local fame. The first to settle here, in 1501, was Sir Peter Newton, builder of the old Council House at Salop; and ere the last scion died out, in 1681, the family had given many High Sheriffs to Shropshire. Sir Isaac Newton, the great philosopher, was connected with the Newtons of Heightley.

The Hall itself has been much altered and modernized; but in the terraced gardens, with their rows of old yew trees, a large fishpond, and some remains of an ancient corn-mill down by the banks of the Camlad, we seem to see traces of a better state of things.

Peeping over the nearer tree-tops, the old grey timeworn tower of its ancient Priory church announces our approach to Chirbury, a picturesque village which can lay claim to a venerable past. Tradition avers that the monastery which once stood here was founded early in the tenth century by Ethelfleda, the 'Lady of the Mercians,' daughter of Alfred the Great; to whom is also attributed the building of Chirbury Castle, which stood at a spot known as 'King's Orchard,' on the outskirts of the village.

In the eleventh of Henry III., a Priory of Black Canons of St. Augustine, established at Snead, a few years previously, by Robert de Boulers, was removed to Chirbury, where it flourished until the Dissolution. Bishop Swinfield twice visited Chirbury Priory in the year 1285, censuring the Prior upon the first occasion for laxity of discipline. His strictures, we may suppose, had the desired effect; for the Bishop subsequently found reason to commend the monks of Chirbury for their almsgiving and piety.

Born at Montgomery Castle in the year 1581, the celebrated Lord Herbert of Chirbury spent much of his time at this place, whence he derived his title. Lord Herbert was created first Baron Chirbury, one of the titles still borne by the Earls of Powis. His literary achievements attracted considerable notice in the reign of James I.

So now let us turn our attention to St. Michael's church, which makes a pleasant picture, its massive western tower soaring above a great yew tree, and roses, ivy and creepers, wreathed about the headstones in the foreground.

The existing parish church is all that remains of the great Priory church of the Austin Canons, 'Llanffynnon-wen,' the 'Church of the Fair Spring,' to give it its poetical Celtic name. A runnel of pure water still rises on the outskirts of the village; and some few years ago a stone water-conduit was brought to light in a garden close to the church.

Though shorn of much of its ancient distinction, Chirbury church is by no means devoid of interest. Owing to neglect and supineness in bygone times, the fabric was fast falling to decay; but of late years the venerable building has been put into a state of thorough repair, thanks to the judicious care of the Rev. John Burd, the present vicar.

The tower door, by which we enter, is surmounted by a small carved figure representing the Virgin and Child. Upon the stone door-jamb are several of those nicks, or scratches, we have puzzled over before—could yonder old yew tree but speak, perchance it might explain that they were caused by sharpening arrows, in the days when long-bows were fashioned from its tough, sinewy limbs.

The interior of Chirbury church is broad, spacious and lofty; for those Austin Friars loved a roomy church to preach in. Owing to the 'spreading' of the roofs, the nave arcades and the walls above lean considerably outwards, though the walls of the aisles are upright; and there are many evidences that, for some reason or other, the present church was 'run up' in a hurry.

There was formerly a fine old roodscreen at Chirbury church; but it was removed many years since to Montgomery. On the wall near the chancel arch we notice a curious tablet to 'Ric Lloid, 1589,' with the Lloyd arms, and a skull, or 'memento mori,' set in a deeply sunk circle. Another small mural tablet displays a shield and the letters

H. M., the initials of Hugh Myddleton, the last Prior of Chirbury. The font, which is large and extremely archaic-looking, was rescued some years ago from a neighbouring garden, where it had long done duty as a water-trough! From its close resemblance to certain ancient holy-water stoups, recently exhibited at Shrewsbury, Mr. Burd, the vicar, considers this font was originally the holy-water stoup of the earlier monastic church.

There is a curious entry in the Parish Book, for the year of grace 1808, which goes to shew it cost more in those days to pay for ale, to assuage the Psalm Singers' thirst, than to defray the cost of their musical instruction! Payment was made, in 1604, to provide 'a bell and cordes to kepe the dogge out of the Churche, in tymes of divine service and preachinge'—autre temps autre mœurs.

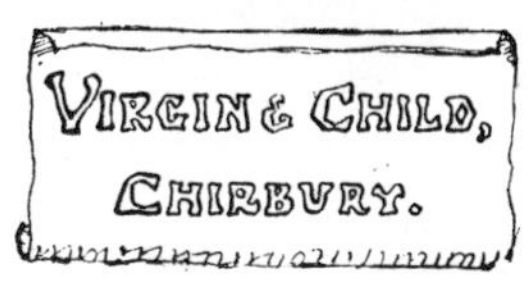

Out in the churchyard, near the vestry door, lie the mortal remains of a former vicar, his brother, and their two wives, whereof the united ages amounted to 378 years, or the respectable average of over 94 years each. A portion of a richly moulded pillar, or rather 'respond,' and some beautiful thirteenth-century floor tiles in the porch of an adjacent house, are remains of the old monkish church.

Some few years ago a small bronze matrix, representing the Virgin and Child, was dug up by chance in Chirbury churchyard, and is now in the possession of the vicar, by whose courtesy we are enabled to give a sketch of a cast from it. The late Mr. Bloxam considered, from the costume and the pose of the figure, that this interesting matrix dates from about the latter part of the fourteenth, or the beginning of the fifteenth century. It is of a kind very rare, if not unique, in this country.

In Chirbury vicarage is preserved a very valuable Library of

Chained Books, probably the most complete private collection of its kind in this country:

> 'Antique Books—rare old Books—
> Gathered from many old corners and nooks!'

The books, 207 in number, treat mainly of theological matters, and are of various dates from 1530 to 1684; most of them retain the iron chains and swivels by which they were fastened in the cabinet. They probably formed part of the library established at Montgomery Castle by George Herbert, the poet and divine; and were transferred to their present resting place by the Rev. Edward Lewis, who, during nearly half of the seventeenth century, was vicar of Chirbury.

Being a man of strong Puritan leanings, Parson Lewis was badly treated by the Royalists. One Sunday morning, when the vicar was in the act of addressing his flock, a troop of horsemen rode into the church, haled the good pastor out of his pulpit, and carried him prisoner to Captain Corbet, who at the time was in command of the King's forces in that locality.

In the secluded rural district around Chirbury, the oldfashioned rustic Stage Plays held their own until the early decades of the present century, long after they had ceased elsewhere; and to this day one may occasionally meet with an ancient greybeard, who in his salad days has figured upon the boards.

These performances generally took place close to some country inn, which, while providing refreshment for the thirsty audience, formed a sort of 'green-room' for the actors themselves. The play, in which two male actors usually took part, was performed, to the scraping of a fiddle, upon a stage improvised for the occasion, by placing some boards upon a couple of farm-waggons borrowed for the purpose.

The plays themselves appear to have been of a simple, not over-refined character, interspersed with broad jokes and scraps of local badinage, to suit the taste of the bucolic audience. 'Prince Mucidorus, or St. George and the Fiery Dragon,' 'Rigs of the Times,' 'Valentine and Orson,' and a piece entitled 'Doctor Forster,' were the favourites.

The hero of the latter is none other than our old acquaintance Faust, and it was supposed to be only acted on the sly, being considered such a very wicked play that something was sure to happen to put a stop to the performance; and the arrival upon the stage of his Satanic Majesty was regarded as the signal for an outbreak of thunder, lightning and hail, if nothing worse.

A mile or so out of Chirbury, in an undulating, well wooded park, on the verge of Marrington Dingle, stands the ancient timbered mansion of Marrington Hall, 'a very noble and sweete place,' as old Pepys would have said. In early documents the name is Maritune, though it was always known to the Welsh as 'Hafod-wen,' the 'Fair Summer Dwelling,' a name as appropriate as pretty, for a more delightful situation for such an 'abode of ancient peace' it would be difficult to imagine.

Ancient Sundial at Marrington.

Embosomed amidst ancestral oaks, under the lee of a range of high, heatherclad hills, this old Elizabethan homestead faces out towards the distant highlands of Montgomery, commanding a prospect of rare extent and beauty. Near one corner of the mansion grows a hollow oak, of enormous bulk and immemorial age, a veritable patriarch among his fellows; while upon the adjacent lawn rises the Sun-dial shewn in our sketch.

This curious Sun-dial, one of the most remarkable of its kind in England, consists of a stone monolith with chamfered edges set upon a large square base, the whole structure being about 5 or 6 feet in height. The figures 1595, cut upon the stone, mark the date of its erection; and around the base runs the inscription: FOR · CHARITI · BID · ME · ADW · WHO · WROUGHT · THIS · STONE · FOR · THE · TOMB · OF · R · LL. A queer figure, carved upon one face of the pillar, may pass for a portrait of Richard Lloyd, the founder; whose arms, with those of the Newtons and other local families, appear upon the shaft.

On the top of the pillar is fixed a sun-dial, or gnomon; while smaller dials were inserted into every nook and cranny whither the sun's rays could penetrate. Upon the shaft are inscribed various suitable mottoes: THESE · SHADES · DO · FLEET · FROM · DAY · TO · DAY; AND · SO · THIS · LIFE · PASSETH · AWAIE: DEUS · MIHI · LUX: FINIS · ITINERIS · SEPULCHRUM: FUI · UT · ES; ERIS · UT · SUM: UT · HORA · SIC · VITA: etc., besides many devices and emblems more or less appropriate to the subject.

In the reign of Henry III., the Manor of Marrington was presented by Sir Robert de Boulers, founder of Chirbury Priory, to a kinsman, and was held for many generations by that ancient family. Passing subsequently to the Lloyds, a Welsh rhymester concocted for the occasion the following curious couplet:

'Lle Bowdler mor ber ar bange,
Yw lle Dafydd Lloyd ifange.'

'Where Bowdler so long had spit and board,
Is now the place of young David Lloyd.'

To vary the route, we will return to Chirbury by way of Marrington Dingle. Here the Camlad has carved out for itself a deep, narrow gorge, running in a due northerly direction; a famous place for wild-flowers, ferns and mosses, which flourish amain beneath the cool shade of the overarching copses, draping with a mantle of luscious verdure the banks of the winding stream.

Tranquil and secluded as is the vale to-day, there are evidences that, in the remote past, Marrington Dingle has proved a bone of contention to successive races of men. Camps and earthworks are planted upon many a salient corner and vantage point; and artificial tumuli abound upon the neighbouring lands.

Rhyd-y-Groes, on the ancient course of the Camlad, tells a different tale; for here, there is reason to believe, the monks in mediæval times stationed their processional cross, while the pilgrims passed through the rippling shallows at Rhyd-y-Groes, the 'Ford of the Cross.'

As we make our way thus towards Chirbury again through these quiet, unfrequented byways, a restful calm, 'hushing the harboured winds,' overspreads the pleasant landscape. The sun has taken his last look at Chirbury, ere we re-enter the village and come to our night's lodging at the Herbert Arms, beneath the shadow of St. Michael's old steeple.

> 'Fresh are the fields, and, like a bloom, they wear
> This delicate evening.'

* * * * * *

Proceeding northwards upon our travels from Chirbury, we cross the Camlad, and, after joining the Newtown road, surmount a low watershed and enter the valley of the Rea. Marton Pool, a good broad sheet of water, comes in view upon the right; and then we pass near Binweston, a diminutive township with an old, faded manor-house, encompassed by a dry moat, and retaining a little oak panelling, but not much else to boast of. Hampton Hall, the seventeenth-century brick mansion of the Whitakers, lies farther away in the same direction.

Grand cumulus clouds, marshalled along the horizon, threaten broken, changeable weather; and a smartish shower now warns us to look out for squalls. But 'for a morning rain leave not y^{r} journey,' as wise old George Herbert has it; so we plod steadily on in the brunt of the breeze, prepared for whatever the Clerk of the Weather may see fit to send our way.

Ere long we come to Worthen, a village of which least said, perhaps, soonest mended; for to our minds the place has little to recommend it. The large parish church is the only building worthy of note, and its attractions are soon exhausted. Worthen Hall, at the farther end of the village, is an early eighteenth-century stuccoed house of unassuming appearance.

Thenceforward we travel along with low, tumbled hills upon our left, while in the opposite quarter we look across the flat Rea valley to the high, wild ridges of the Stiperstones, whose flanks, still shaggy with woodland, formed a royal hunting forest under the Saxon kings.

At Aston Rogers we take a glance at the Pound House, a rather shabby-looking timbered cottage of late fifteenth-century date, with remains of a circular moat; and anon we diverge from our route to visit the site of Caurse Castle.

A stiff climb through a tangle of brushwood brings us to the steep, green mounds, whereon the castle stood, though but little of it remains save a few fragments of rough, weedgrown masonry. So far as one can gather therefrom, the building took the form of a parallelogram, which adapted itself to the natural trend of the ridge, and appears to have had a round-tower at each corner. At the highest point stood the keep; and a well, supplied by the stream hard by, lay somewhere within the enceinte. The position must have been a strong one, in days when artillery was in its infancy; and it commanded the avenues of approach in every direction.

Caurse Castle was founded by Roger Fitz Corbet, one of William's Norman knights, very soon after the Conquest; and, from its exposed situation, must have formed a salient point in the series of border strongholds, which the Normans drew around these Shropshire Marches. After having been taken and burned by the Welsh, the castle was re-captured and garrisoned for Henry II., in 1165. Long afterwards the place passed to the Barons Stafford, and was eventually captured, and its defences 'slighted' by the Parliamentarians, in 1645.

Away to the westward looms a wild, hilly, sparsely peopled region, known in olden times as Causeland. 'This Causeland,' to use John Leland's phrase, 'sumtyme longinge to the Duke of Buckyngham, crooketh mervelously about the upper Parts of Shropeshire.' It still maintains its isolated character, though the forest that once overspread this portion of the county has long since ceased to exist.

Leaving Caurse Castle behind us, we next bend our steps towards Westbury, whose church, though of ancient origin, has been shockingly modernized. In the churchyard there is a curious epitaph to one

Edward Gittins, a local blacksmith, who probably composed the effusion himself.

Marche-manor Farm, the subject of the adjoining sketch, lies in a secluded dell, not far from Westbury. It is an ancient place, with a beautiful oak parlour lighted by long, low, lattice-paned windows; and contains a richly carved and panelled mantelpiece. Staircase, floors, rafters, all are of heart-of-oak; shewing how plentiful was the 'Shropshire weed' in the early days of the seventeenth century, when the

house was built. Marche-manor formed part of the great Barony of Caurse Castle, and was held by the Fitz Corbets under Roger de Montgomery, the Conqueror's vicegerent; but it is one of those places which are blessed in not having a history.

The trees and shrubberies, by which the old place is surrounded, set off to great advantage its ancient timbered gables. A pretty lakelet close at hand is a favourite haunt of wildfowl; and the soft fluting of coots and waterhens, hunting among the reeds, makes a pleasant accompaniment as we sit a-sketching here.

Crossing the Welshpool road, as it traverses Wattlesborough Heath—nowadays a heath no longer—we press on to Great Woolaston; whose unpretentious, eighteenth-century chapel, otherwise not specially attractive, contains one memorial of the past familiar to many Salopians.

OLD THOMAS PARR.

FROM A PRINT PUBLISHED IN 1802.

This is a certain brass plate, set into the wall, and bearing engraved upon its surface the portrait here shewn, with the following inscription: 'THE OLD, OLD, VERY OLD MAN, THOMAS PARR, was Born at the Glyn, in the Township of Winnington, within This Chapelry of Great Willaston, and Parish of Alberbury, in the County of Salop, In the Year of our Lord 1483. He lived in the Reigns of Ten Kings and Queens of England (viz.), K. Edwd 4th, K. Edwd 5th, K. Rich^{d} 3rd, K. Hen. 7th, K. Hen. 8th, K. Edwd 6th, Q. Mary, Q. Eliz., K. James 1st, and K. Chas 1st. Died the 13th and was buryed in Westminster Abby on the 15th of November, 1635; Aged 152 Years and 9 months.'

Taylor, the 'Water Poet,' writing in the year 1635, in a work entitled 'The Olde, Olde, very Olde Man,' tells us Thomas Parr was an early riser, sober and industrious, and thus describes his appearance when advanced in years:

> 'Though old age his face with wrinkles fill,
> Hee hath been handsome, and is comely still;
> Well-faced, and though his Beard not oft corrected,
> Yet neate it grows, not like a beard neglected.'

Braggington Hall, Shropshire.

All sorts of tales were current concerning this famous centenarian. It is said that when the Cockneys, having heard of his renown, came to seek for Old Parr to carry him before the King, they addressed themselves to a very aged man whom they supposed to be Thomas Parr; and were not a little astonished when he replied, 'Oh, it ain't me, Lor' bless yer, it's my *father* as you wants!'

That unfortunate visit to London, indeed, seems to have undermined the old man's constitution; and who knows but that, had he stayed snugly at home in his native Shropshire, Thomas Parr might have been alive and hearty to this day.

Left a widower at the age of 122, our hero sought consolation in the arms of a fair daughter of Wales. Yet three years later, we hear of this ancient Lothario doing penance at Alberbury church, for having broken his marriage vow in an intrigue with a certain frail maid named Catherine Milton.

As the story goes, when brought before Charles I., the King, congratulating Thomas upon so long outrunning the allotted span, demanded what else he had done to boast of. Old Parr, taken aback by the question, could think of nothing better than his affair with Catherine Milton; whereupon His Majesty exclaimed, 'Oh fie, Thomas, fie! can you remember nothing but your vices?'

But to resume. Beyond Woolaston, in an outlying nook of the county, we happen upon the fine old Jacobean mansion called Braggington. As may be gathered from our sketch, it is a massive brick-and-stone edifice, with mullioned windows and tall, steep gables, surmounted by stone finials. From the recessed central bay projects the main portal, with its weatherworn stone pillars, and architrave displaying the date 1674, and oak, nailstudded door. Large, elaborately ornamented leaden spout-heads, are seen on each side below the roof. A broad old oak staircase, with massive newels bearing the device of some ancient family, is the most prominent feature inside; the place having gone much to decay, and being now used as a farmhouse.

Out in the garden they are hiving the bees, and the beating of kettles and frying-pans makes a quaint, odd, tinkling sound, like the strains of a toy symphony, as we take our leave.

From Braggington we ramble on to Coedway, and soon lose ourselves once more among cool, leafy corners and crankling nooks, where Nature reigns untended:

> 'Give to me the life I love,
> Let the lave go by me,
> Give the jolly heavens above,
> And the byway nigh me.'

Yonder a few miles away rise the Breidden Hills, 'brewing the weather, like a Lapland witch,' and looking wonderfully mountainous for their inches; with lights and shadows chasing each other athwart their wooded flanks, and their summits wreathed in a cope of lowering storm cloud. These hills, indeed, have a reputation to sustain in the matter of meteorology, as their name Breith-hin, 'Broken-weather,' obviously indicates.

Rising abruptly from Severn-side to a height of 1,324 feet, this isolated range is a conspicuous landmark for many a mile around, keeping watch and ward over the broad Vale of Shrewsbury, much as Gibraltar Rock guards the entrance to the Mediterranean. An upthrow of volcanic rock has here thrust the local strata aside, and by its intrusion has produced the picturesque, broken scenery, found upon the flanks of the range.

Like most of these border heights, the Breidden Hills are crowned by camps and ancient 'castells'; while some authorities have located the scene of Caractacus's last battle amidst their rocky fastnesses. Cefn-y-Castell, near Moel-y-Golta, the highest point of the range, is a good example of an early British earthwork; and Bausley Hill, an eastern spur, is the supposed site of a Roman station, in connection with the ford across the Severn at the western foot of the Breiddens. Offa's Dyke traverses the country in the same quarter. Rodney's Pillar, a memento of that hero's naval victories, is a noticeable object from afar, crowning the summit of an isolated peak.

Just across the Welsh border, we find the Old Hand and Diamond Inn at Coedway, a quiet little roadside house, near the junction of Severn and Vyrnwy, whither fishermen resort for the sport on those well-known waters. Mine host is himself an ardent devotee of 'the gentle art,' and a guide and counsellor of no mean calibre in matters piscatorial.

Close beside the Vyrnwy, a few miles hence, stands Melverley, about the most un-come-at-able village in Shropshire; 'Melverley, God help us!' is the local phrase, which sufficiently explains its own meaning. Yet they say if you ask a native whence he hails, he will reply, 'Whoy from Melverley, wheer else?' as though not to know Melverley argued oneself unknown.

Duly rested and refreshed we now set forth from Coedway, and, passing the Prince's Oak, a memento of King George the Fourth, we follow a road that gives us pretty peeps of Loton Park and its handsome red-brick Hall, the residence of Sir Bryan Leighton, whose forbears have been seated here since the Conqueror's time.

Close under the lee of Loton Park nestles the diminutive village of Alberbury, a quiet, old-world looking spot, innocent of any 'public;' and where Her Majesty's postal affairs are conducted by the universal provider who runs the one and only shop. But Alberbury church, the subject of our next illustration, will well repay a visit.

It is a structure of many different dates, and has all the charm that such variety lends. The Loton Chapel, seen in the front of the picture, was built about the year 1340, its windows having the rather intricate tracery in vogue about that time. Overhead we get a glimpse of the tower, a work of earlier date, with its curious, steep, saddle-backed roof, and primitive weather-vane. The east end of the chancel, the oldest part of the church, is pure Norman work.

An ancient churchyard cross with tall, slender shaft, backed by the sombre verdure of some yew trees, adds a pleasing feature to the scene.

The south aisle, used time out of mind as a chapel by the Leightons of Loton Hall, has a richly ornamented open-timber roof, with cherubs' heads cut upon the brackets that support it; and the massive old carved oak benches, black with age, should not be overlooked. Quite out of the common, also, are the windows already referred to, with their peculiar geometrical tracery, and scraps of fourteenth-century glass.

An ugly barrel-vaulted ceiling evidently disguises the original timbered roof of the nave, one principal whereof is still visible at the west end, with its big stone supporting corbels. The chancel is lighted by two semi-headed windows, surmounted by a circular light, all of

Norman date; and some fine brasses and mural tablets, to the Leightons and the Lysters, are seen here and there about the interior.

'By Alberbyri Chirche,' notes Leland, 'appere the Ruines of Fulk Guarine the noble Warriar's Castel.' The remains of this early, thirteenth-century stronghold, rise a stone's throw south-westward from the church; but they are so fragmentary and devoid of detail as to have little attraction for the antiquary; indeed, one crumbling ivy-mantled tourelle is about the sum-total of the fabric.

Alberbury Priory, an establishment of Benedictine monks, founded by Fulk Fitz-Warine early in the thirteenth century, is represented by a few Gothic fragments in a farmhouse called White Abbey, close to the Severn, a long mile north-east of the village. The principal remains are the groined ceiling of the chapel, which springs from stone corbels, and has curious carvings, at the intersections of the ribs, representing the Agnus Dei, a monk's head, and an angel wrestling with the Evil One; and one or two good pointed doorways in the lower story. The monastery was suppressed in Henry the Sixth's reign, when the estate was granted to All Souls' College, Oxford.

Turning our backs upon the Severn, which here flows along in easy curves between low, red, clayey banks, we now pass through a pair of tall iron gates near Alberbury church, and make our way viâ Loton Deer Park to Wattlesborough Castle.

The walk across the Park introduces us to some picturesque bits of woodland relieved by rough, rocky dingles, where old gnarled hawthorns and hazel bushes thrive amain; while from the higher reaches of the Park there is a varied prospect over the neighbouring country-side, half English in its snug, cultivated lowlands, half Welsh where the shaggy hills loom stern and wild.

Arrived at Wattlesborough, our tramp is rewarded by the sight of the curious old farmhouse shewn in the sketch over page. In the centre, surrounded by buildings of no particular age, rises a low, massive, quadrangular tower of good ashlar masonry, with the flat buttresses characteristic of Norman work, and one or two windows of later date.

This tower, with portions of a projecting wing, formed part of the original Castle, and is very solidly constructed, the tower walls measuring as much as 7 or 8 feet in thickness. A circular stone stairway leads up to the several stages, some of the chambers retaining their rude stone fireplaces, and other simple contrivances; while on the topmost floor is a sort of closet, or prison-hole, and certain slanting ledges on the wall indicating the position of an earlier and lower roof.

There are said to have formerly been three other towers at Wattlesborough Castle, but that they were pulled down to provide stones for building the Loton Chapel, at Alberbury. Be that as it may, the Castle certainly seems to have covered more ground at one time; and the sites of two moats, a watch-tower and drawbridge, are pointed out in an orchard on the western side of the farmhouse.

Planted upon an outlying spur of the Breidden Hills, Wattlesborough must have held a position of some strategic importance,

WATTLESBOROUGH CASTLE.

controlling with Alberbury Castle the passes of the Severn, and the road into Wales between this and Caurse Castle.

Of its history, so far as we are aware, there is little to be said. A Fitz-Corbet held Wattlesborough under Roger de Montgomery, at the time of Domesday Survey. In after years the Castle passed to the de la Poles, and the de Burghs, coming eventually by marriage to the Leighton family, whose property it remains to this day. Wattlesborough is reputed to be one of the few estates which have never been bartered for 'filthy lucre,' since the days when the Normans first lorded it over English land.

With shadows lengthening before us, we now set our faces towards Shrewsbury. Half an hour's tramp brings us near Rowton Castle, the

THE SHELTON OAK.

Rutunium, as some assert, of Roman days. Then we catch a glimpse of Cardeston Church away to the south, and presently pass under the viaduct which carries the defunct Potteries line across the highway. Ford village, whose church boasts a fine old roodscreen, is but a mile distant towards the north, with Shrawardine castle-mound keeping it in countenance on the farther bank of Severn.

On past Dunthall and Onslow Hall, the erstwhile abode of the renowned Mr. Speaker Onslow, we bowl along the dusty highway with homeward-bound Salopians, until, some two miles short of our journey's end, we call a halt to take a look at the Shelton Oak, one of the 'lions' of the locality.

Yonder it stands, a storm-rent relic of the immemorial past, holding its own bravely yet ''gainst the tooth of time and razure of oblivion,' though bereft of many a stalwart limb by the gales of a thousand winters.

This venerable tree still rears aloft its gaunt, grey, wrinkled branches, lifeless now, save for some ragged foliage that yet clings around the lower part of the trunk. The latter has become hollow inside, where a sort of paved chamber affords standing-room for perhaps a dozen people.

As seen in our sketch, a sturdy prop, itself a fair-sized tree, serves to buttress the old giant upon the side towards which he inclines.

According to a time-honoured tradition, the Welsh Prince, Owen Glendower, climbed up amidst the branches of the Shelton Oak, in order to watch thence how the fortunes of war progressed during the famous Battle of Shrewsbury:

> 'The bloody rout that gave
> To Harry's brow a wreath—to Hotspur's heart a grave.'

Soon after leaving the Shelton Oak, the towers and steeples of the County-town put in an appearance ahead; here and there a country house is seen, overlooking the Severn as it winds through the vale, and bricks and mortar begin to usurp the place of trim green fields and hedgerows. That red-brick mansion upon yonder bank is The Mount, birthplace of that very distinguished Salopian, the late Charles Darwin.

Anon we descend a hill, and enter the 'antient streete callyd Frainckarell this many a daye,' a transpontine suburb of Shrewsbury, deriving its name from the fact that, in earlier days, its denizens were exempted from payment of certain tolls levied upon their neighbours over the water.

Across the street rises a group of half-timbered houses, whose quaint congeries of beetling gables, chequered beams, lattice-paned casements, and dark, timeworn archways, make an old-world picture. More ancient still, perhaps, is the long, low, two-storied house front a little farther on; its massive old moulded cornices black with age, and curious louvred lights in the upper story—a venerable specimen.

A MAIDEN GARLAND FROM MINSTERLEY.

And here at last is the Welsh Bridge, in Leland's time the 'greatest, fayrest, and highest Bridge upon Severne Streame.' At that period, as Leland tells us, the Bridge had 'six great Arches of stone, with a great gate at one end of it to enter by into the Towne, and at the other end towardes Wales a mighty stronge Towre, to prohibit Enimies to enter into the bridge.'

Old paintings and woodcuts shew it to have been an extremely picturesque structure, with bold buttresses, and narrow, pointed arches; and a tall, machicolated tower, with frowning gateway, portcullis, and mailed figure of King Edward IV. keeping guard at the western end of the Bridge—a subject worthy the brush of a James Holland, or a Samuel Prout.

* * * * * *

So now, with our arrival at Shrewsbury, we have completed the circuit of our Shropshire wanderings. The subject treated of is so wide, so varied, and of such many-sided interest, that one can do little more than scratch the ground, so to speak, within the compass of a volume such as this. But we venture to hope that the perusal of these pages may lead others to explore this pleasant land for themselves; and it only remains for us to bid farewell to the gentle reader, by whose courtesy we have rambled thus far together amidst the 'Nooks and Corners of Shropshire.'

SHREWSBURY.

INDEX

THE END.

Elliot Stock, 62, Paternoster Row, London.

REST PRAY SLEEP
GRH

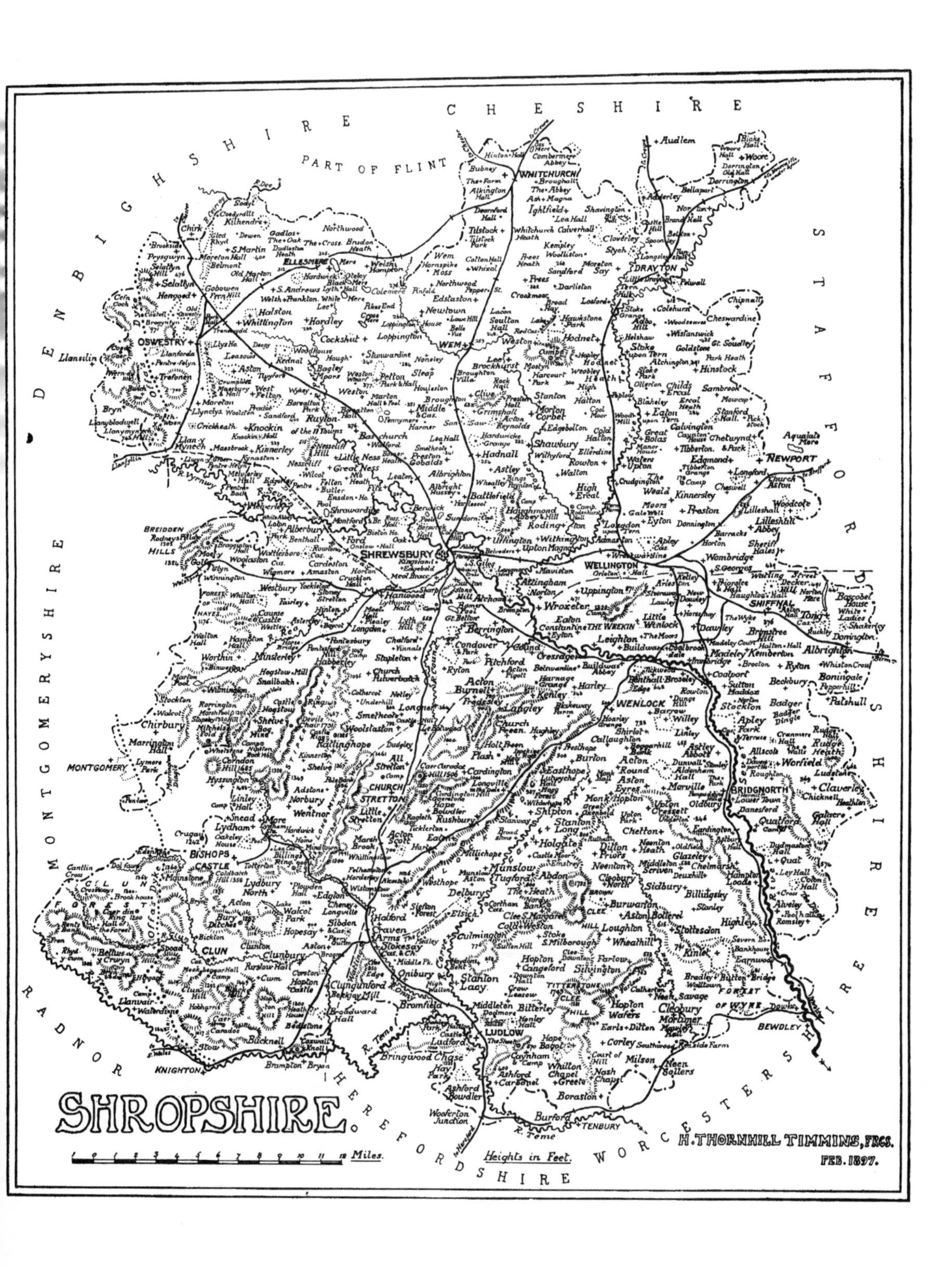

SHROPSHIRE.
H. THORNHILL TIMMINS, FRGS.
FEB. 1897.
Miles.
Heights in Feet.
CHESHIRE
DENBIGHSHIRE
PART OF FLINT
STAFFORDSHIRE
MONTGOMERYSHIRE
RADNOR
HEREFORDSHIRE
WORCESTERSHIRE
WHITCHURCH
ELLESMERE
OSWESTRY
WEM
DRAYTON
NEWPORT
SHREWSBURY
WELLINGTON
SHIFFNAL
WENLOCK
BRIDGNORTH
CHURCH STRETTON
BISHOPS CASTLE
CLUN
LUDLOW
MONTGOMERY
KNIGHTON
TENBURY
BEWDLEY
THE WREKIN
CLUN FOREST
FOREST OF WYRE